MSU LIBRARIES
P9-DEC-950

A SURVEY OF ENGLISH DICTIONARIES

By

M. M. MATHEWS

NEW YORK / RUSSELL & RUSSELL

1966

FIRST PUBLISHED IN 1933
REISSUED, 1966, BY RUSSELL & RUSSELL
A DIVISION OF ATHENEUM HOUSE, INC.
L.C. CATALOG CARD NO. 65—17912

REPRINTED FROM A COPY IN THE COLLECTIONS OF
THE MORRIS R. COHEN LIBRARY OF THE
CITY COLLEGE OF NEW YORK

PRINTED IN THE UNITED STATES OF AMERICA

PREFACE

A DICTIONARY of some kind is usually the reference book which a student uses earliest and longest. It is, as a rule, the only work of the kind which he purchases and continues to make some use of after the days of his formal schooling are over. Many of the students with whom I come in contact, however, are not sufficiently acquainted with dictionaries to have much interest in them, or to get from them the full amount of help which they afford. Students frequently fail to discriminate between dictionaries, but consult the nearest available one for information that lies more within the special province of some other similar work. In writing this book I have tried to give a brief account of English lexicography, and to enumerate some of the chief characteristics of the English dictionaries in common use. If my treatment of the subject tends to stimulate interest in dictionaries or to supply something of an intelligent background for their appreciative use, I shall be pleased.

It is a great pleasure to record here my thanks to Sir William Craigie for his most generous encouragement and for his never-failing assistance with the work. My thanks are also due to Mr. George Watson, whose painstaking criticisms have been very helpful.

M. M. M.

CAMBRIDGE
MASSACHUSETTS

CONTENTS

I

THE ENGLISH VOCABULARY

THE following chapters deal with books which sum up in one way or another the English vocabulary. It will be well, therefore, to take some account here of a few of the main facts bearing on the phenomenal growth which the vocabulary has undergone within the past thousand years.

For many centuries after the English language had come into being, it was spoken by a comparatively small number of people. In its earliest form, now called either Old English or Anglo-Saxon, it was the speech of some Germanic peoples who came to England after A.D. 450, having been invited over from their continental homes to give military assistance to some of the inhabitants of Britain. These newcomers were the Angles, the Saxons, and the Jutes (or Frisians, according to one early authority). The Angles and the Saxons were more numerous than the others, and have their names preserved in the expression 'Anglo-Saxon'.

The exact extent of the Anglo-Saxon vocabulary is not known. Scholars are certain that the entire vocabulary is not exhibited in the records that have survived to the present day. Through the loss of many manuscripts a part at least of the vocabulary has perished. No doubt there were also many words that were not recorded in Anglo-Saxon writings, and have consequently escaped the diligence of those who have made dictionaries of Anglo-Saxon. Enough of the vocabulary has been preserved, however, to require two substantial-sized volumes to do it justice in the largest dictionary of Anglo-Saxon now available.

Anglo-Saxon, though it was employed by Germanic tribes, was not composed altogether of Germanic words. There had been taken over into the vocabulary a very few Celtic words which the Anglo-Saxons borrowed from the British, and a much larger number of Latin terms. The Germanic peoples who came over to England in the fifth century had already had some contact with Roman civilization and had taken in from Latin a few words such as those which appear in modern English as *street, wall, chalk, camp, mile, wine.* When the Angles and Saxons and Jutes reached England they were associated with Latin-speaking Britons who had been brought up under Roman rulership. From these Britons the Anglo-Saxons borrowed some more Latin words.

When the Anglo-Saxons had been in England about a century and a half missionaries under St. Augustine came and began a religious conquest of the island which resulted, among other things, in the taking over into Anglo-Saxon of still more Latin words, many of them ecclesiastical terms. A fairly large number of these church terms were not native Latin words, but simply Greek words in Latin spellings. Among these were *abbot, apostle, deacon, hymn, pope, bishop, monk, nun,* in the forms which they had at that early time.

Toward the close of the eighth century, in A.D. 787, Scandinavian sea-rovers began to harry the northern coast of England. Within the next two centuries and a half the Danes had succeeded in taking possession of half of England and in placing over their kingdom a Danish king, Canute (1017–35). It is surprising that these Scandinavian inroads into such large areas of England did not threaten the very existence of Anglo-Saxon. The result of these invasions, however, was not at all disastrous to the supremacy of that speech. Many Scandinavian words became embedded in the native language, and thus the Anglo-

Saxon vocabulary was made more composite than ever. It was not until after the Middle English period (*c.* 1100–1500) had set in that the native language began to show a decided Scandinavian element. Words like *awe, both, call, cast, get, raise, scare, skin, sly, swain, thwart, window,* are derived from Scandinavian.

In 1066 an event of much greater importance for the native English vocabulary took place. This event was the Norman invasion. The number of followers that William the Conqueror brought with him into England is not known. Probably his army numbered not more than fifteen thousand, but during the twenty years following the Battle of Hastings many thousand Flemings, Picards, Normans, and Burgundians came over into Britain. All of these new comers spoke French in some form or other. They did not care to learn Anglo-Saxon, and many of the native Englishmen forsook their own speech and used French instead. No schools survived in which the native speech was cultivated. Very few literary works were produced in Anglo-Saxon, and in the few that were written it is easy to see that French words were penetrating into the vocabulary. French was the language of culture and polite society. Anglo-Saxon was for about two centuries confined largely to rustics.

The supremacy of French did not endure permanently, of course. After a while the tide began to turn in favour of the native tongue. During the reign of Henry III (1216–72) a nationalistic movement was under way which must have contributed to the dignifying of the old native language. There was in the early part of the thirteenth century a number of writers at work whose aim was to instruct the common people. For accomplishing this object they wrote in the native vernacular rather than in French.

The English which appeared in the writings of the thirteenth century was quite different in vocabulary from that which had existed a few centuries earlier. A great part of the old vocabulary had disappeared entirely and hundreds of words from French had come in. A great many of these early borrowings from French still remain in the language. Among them are such words as *chaste, cruel, coward, dangerous, devout, false, foolhardy, jealous, gentle, hardy, humble, mountain, noble, obedient, religious, simple, tender*, &c. The influence of French on English continued vigorously for several centuries. This borrowing from different varieties of French at various times accounts for related words in English like *gaol, jail*; *royal, realm*; *wallop, gallop*; *wage, gage*, &c.

The borrowings from French that began with the Norman Conquest in 1066 naturally added impetus to direct borrowings from Latin, which was the source of the greater part of the French vocabulary. During the fifteenth and sixteenth centuries there were hundreds of words taken over directly from Latin. Some of these had already been borrowed from French or were taken over likewise in their French forms. This helter-skelter, hit or miss, borrowing, sometimes from written Latin, sometimes from French of one sort or another, enriched the English vocabulary with many words, some of them being closely related, as *chieftain, captain*; *conceive, concept*; *danger, domination*; *daunt, indomitable*; *fay, fate*; *feat, fact*; *fealty, fidelity*; *grief, grave*; *leal, legal*; *peace, pacify*; *poison, potion*; *sign, signal*; *strait, strict*, and many others.

It is easy to see that by the year 1600 the English vocabulary was a complex one, containing native Germanic words like *arm, hand, land*, along with other words from Scandinavian, Greek, Latin, French, &c. But since 1600 English has been augmented in such a variety of ways that in a brief sketch like this we can attempt no more than to point out a few of the most important things that have affected the vocabulary.

Early in the seventeenth century English colonists came to America and began to live in surroundings that greatly influenced their language. In the first place, these colonists had contacts sooner or later with the native Indians and with people from many different parts of the world. One result of this mingling of many peoples in America was the bringing into the English vocabulary of a large number of new words. From the North American Indians have come such words as *caribou, catalpa, chinquapin, chipmunk, hickory, hominy, moose, mugwump, papoose, pecan, pemmican, persimmon, pone, possum, powwow, raccoon, sachem, sagamore, samp, scuppernong, skunk, squaw, Tammany, terrapin, toboggan, tomahawk, totem, tuckahoe,* &c.

From contact with Dutch colonists in America English-speaking settlers added to the resources of their language such words as *boss, bowery, caboose, patroon, pea-jacket, Santa Claus, scow, slaw, sleigh, snoop, spook, stoop* (of a house), *waffle.* Spanish in the same way contributed words like *adobe, arroyo, bronco, calaboose, chaparral, cinch, coyote, lariat, loco, mesa, mescal, mesquite, monte, mustang, peon, pinto, quirt,* &c.

About the time English colonists were coming to America English trading companies were sending ships to India. Early in the seventeenth century there were words from India making their appearance in English. Some of these early borrowings are *calico, chintz, gingham.* Colonists soon followed the traders into those distant regions, and there now exist in English many words of Indian, Malay, and Australian origin. Some of these are *amuck, anaconda, bamboo, boomerang, cheroot, cockatoo, dingo, dugong, dumdum, loot, monsoon, nabob, pariah, sepoy, shawl, teak, toddy.* Within the past three hundred years English explorers and colonists have had dealings of some sort with practically all the major races on the earth, and one result of this wide range of contacts is the appearance in English of words from all quarters of the globe.

In addition to the physical contacts just mentioned, English people have felt the influence of cultural associations with other peoples. From Italy and France have come many words pertaining to music, architecture, &c. The following are a few examples: *adagio, allegro, andante, balcony, colonnade, concerto, cornice, corridor, duet, falsetto, finale, fresco, improvisatore, libretto, madrigal, opera, operetta, parapet, piano, piazza, piccolo, pilaster, quartet, soprano, stanza, tempo, terra-cotta, torso, violin.*

It is not necessary to go further in this rapid review of a few of the more outstanding ways in which the English vocabulary has come to its present fullness. To tell in full the story of the vocabulary would be to write a book many times larger than this one, and to enumerate a surprisingly large number of kinds of words that appear in English. Consider, for example, the words which English has derived from the names of persons. Among the words of this group we have *ampere, bowie knife, boycott, dahlia, derrick, derringer, gerrymander, guy, lynch, mackintosh, mesmerize, ohm, poinsettia, sandwich, shrapnel, volt, watt, wistaria.*

Every conquest which English-speaking people have achieved in the material or intellectual realm has resulted in an enlargement of the English vocabulary. A full account, therefore, of the vocabulary would be a summing up of the progress of the Anglo-Saxon race in all the realms wherein its members have laboured. The story of our vocabulary would also be the story of how the speech of a few tribes once living around the mouth of the Elbe River, on the borderland of the present Denmark and Germany, has spread over the earth and has become the chief method of communication employed by approximately two hundred million persons.

The expansion of the English vocabulary has furnished

the chief motive for the making of dictionaries from early times to the present. As long as the vocabulary continues to grow, that is, as long as English continues to be a living language, new dictionaries will be necessary to record the ever-growing vocabulary.

II

DICTIONARIES BEFORE 1600

STUDENTS of a foreign language not infrequently write in the margins of their books, or between the lines, translations or explanations of difficult words occurring in the text. This practice is very old. Students in England in the seventh century indulged in it, and by so doing they laid the remote foundations of later lexicographic activities. To this day there have survived numerous manuscripts which show the words and explanations, *glosses*, we call them, written in to elucidate the text. Most of the works so glossed are in Latin, and the glosses are sometimes in Latin and sometimes in Anglo-Saxon.

At an early date, certainly by the eighth century, there grew up the custom of making *glossae collectae*, i.e. collections of glosses. In a monastery there would be a fairly large number of Latin works that had been glossed. Monastic teachers or students would go through these, listing all the glosses as they occurred. Such a collection, a *glossarium* or *glossary*, was very useful to students, being for them a sort of dictionary.

One of these glossaries has come down to us in several manuscripts. The collection in its earliest form is found in two continental manuscripts, forming variants, which are called the Epinal and Erfurt Glossaries, because they are preserved one at Epinal in East France, and the other at Erfurt, in Thüringen in Germany. The same collection exists in a fuller form in a large handsome manuscript belonging to Corpus Christi College, Cambridge, and consequently known as the Corpus Glossary. This manuscript is believed to have been written about A.D. 725. The entries number over two thousand, and are in an alphabetical order which has regard for only the two initial letters of the words treated.

In the last decades of the tenth century Ælfric, later abbot of Eynsham, near Oxford, produced a Latin grammar to which he added a short classified Latin-English dictionary, the first of its kind. This seems to have been expanded sometime in the eleventh century into the form known as Abbot Ælfric's Glossary. This glossary begins with the Latin words pertaining to the implements of agriculture, then comes a collection of political terms, and next there is a list of a hundred words denoting animals. Other groups are devoted to names of insects, birds, plants, trees, arms, drinks, clothing, games, colours, winds, ships, grains, &c.

There are in existence many other collections of glosses prepared before the fifteenth century. In 1857 Thomas Wright, the noted antiquarian, made an interesting collection of some of these Anglo-Saxon vocabularies, and this was revised and enlarged in 1884 by Professor R. P. Wül(c)ker. It is interesting to look over some of the old word-lists in this work. Many words still in every-day use, such as *box*, *flood*, *garlic*, *hazel-nut*, *hood*, *fosterfather*, *stepmother*, *nightingale*, *rib*, *handle*, appear in an eighth-century vocabulary. In a vocabulary of the eleventh century the word *bigamus* (=bigamist) occurs, and the definition given is 'uir unius mulieris', the husband of one woman. In this same work there is a vocabulary, believed to be of the fifteenth century, which is embellished with numerous drawings that illustrate, after a fashion, the various classes of words dealt with in the vocabulary. These drawings are so numerous as immediately to suggest the illustrated dictionaries of a much later date.

It is easy to see that in the later vocabularies in Wright-Wül(c)ker the Latin used in the explanations of the entries gradually gives way to English. The object was no longer to confine attention altogether to the explanation of difficult Latin words, but to give English equivalents of as many of these as possible. The changes slowly made were in the direction of providing a dictionary of Latin for the use of English-speaking students.

About the middle of the fifteenth century appeared two important works of a lexicographic nature. One of these compilations was the *Ortus* (i.e. Hortus) *Vocabulorum*, based upon an earlier *Medulla Grammatice*, or *Grammatices*. The *Ortus* enjoys the distinction of having been the first Latin-English dictionary printed in England (London, 1500). A Dominican friar, Galfridus Grammaticus, or Geoffrey the Grammarian, is believed to have been the author who produced about 1440 an English-Latin vocabulary. In 1499 Pynson issued the first printed edition of this work, which was called *Promptorium parvulorum sive clericorum*. This 'Children's Store-room', or 'Repository', is significant in that it indicates clearly the shift of emphasis in the preparation of such vocabularies. Former vocabularies and glossaries had adopted the Latin-English order of arrangement, their primary emphasis being the elucidation of Latin. In the *Promptorium* the English precedes the Latin. The nine or ten thousand entries in Geoffrey's work are mainly nouns and verbs, the nouns being in one alphabet and the verbs in another. A few words belonging to other parts of speech are included. The first entry, for example, is *Abakke* (aback) an adverb, and the second is *Abashd* (abashed), a participle.

In the sixteenth century there appeared more vocabularies and dictionaries than we need take full account of here. Among such works of the century as possess especial interest the following may be enumerated. In 1514 John Palsgrave, a native of London who had studied at Cambridge and at Paris, was serving as tutor to Princess Mary, sister of Henry VIII, and went with her to France on the occasion of her marriage to Louis XII. Palsgrave wrote for the help of his royal pupil a book in which he attempted to reduce the French language to grammatical rules. The larger part of this treatise, which appeared in 1530 with the title *Lesclarcissement de la langue francoyse*, was an English-French vocabulary. It was said of Palsgrave that he asked Pynson, his printer, not to sell the book promiscuously, 'lest his proffit by teching the Frenche tonge myght be mynished by the sale of the same to suche persons as, besids hym, wern disposed to studye the sayd tongue'. This work was the forerunner of others of a similar nature that came later in the century. William Salesbury in 1547 produced what he called a *Dictionary in Englyshe and Welshe*, though the arrangement was Welsh-English. In 1591 Richard Percival brought out a dictionary of Spanish and English. An Italian-English dictionary by Florio appeared in 1598.

The Dictionary of Syr Thomas Eliot knyght appeared in 1538 and passed through several editions before the author's death in 1546. It was a Latin-English dictionary and was dedicated to Henry VIII. In the dedication Elyot stated that with the aid of his dictionary students of Latin could make more progress in six months 'than they mought haue doone afore in thre yeres, withoute perfyte instructours, whyche are not many, and suche as be, are not easy to come by'.

Thomas Cooper, Fellow of Magdalen College, Oxford, brought out enlargements of Elyot's dictionary in 1548, 1552, and 1559. Cooper's most important lexicographical work, however, was his *Thesaurus Linguæ Romanæ & Britannicæ*, published in 1565. It is said that after Cooper had spent eight years collecting material for his dictionary, his wife, fearing that he might kill himself with study, burned all his notes, making it necessary for him to work eight years longer in finishing his *Thesaurus*. When the work appeared one of his critics insinuated that he had copied it verbatim from a thesaurus that had recently been brought out by Robert Stephens (Estienne), a French scholar. Cooper had really based his work upon that of Stephens, and had availed himself of whatever help Elyot's dictionary afforded, but he had made contributions of his own. The *Thesaurus* found favour with Queen Elizabeth, and contributed to Cooper's preferment at her hands.

The *Abcedarium Anglico Latinum, pro Tyrunculis*, by Richard Huloet, or Howlet, was, as its title shows, a work designed to be of service to those beginning the study of Latin. It appeared in 1552. Huloet in compiling his dictionary leaned quite heavily on Elyot's dictionary of 1538. He took a great many of Elyot's entries that were Latin-English and made them English-Latin. For example, Elyot (1538) has

Pullatio, hatchynge of chyckens.
Pullicies, a bryngynge forthe or hatchynge of chyckens.

In Huloet (1552) these become

Hatchynge of chickens, *Pullatio*, *Pullities*.

The following entries in the *Abcedarium* (1552) are founded on Elyot:

Cockatryce whyche is a Serpente, called the kynge of serpentes, whose nature is to kyll wyth hyssynge onelye, *Basiliscus regulus*.

Gentleman of the first head, or *Ironice* to be applyed to such as would be estemed a gentleman, hauing no poynt or qualitie of a gentleman, nor gentleman borne. . . . It is sayde that *Vir trium literarium* is a thiefe, bicause it [i.e. the Latin word for *thief*] is written with 3 letters, *f.u.r*.

Twenty years after the first appearance of Huloet's dictionary, John Higgins, divine, schoolmaster, and editor of *The Mirror for Magistrates*, brought out a second edition of it very much enlarged and altered. Higgins added

French equivalents to the Latin ones already in Huloet. The method employed by Higgins in getting out his edition of the *Abcedarium* is indicated in the introductory part of the work. Higgins writes: 'For ye better attayning to the knowledge of words, I went not to the common Dictionaries only, but also to the Authors themselues . . . and finallye I wrate not in the whole Booke one quyre, without perusinge and conference of many Authors.'

In 1570 Peter Levins, a Fellow of Magdalen College, Oxford, produced a curious work which he called *Manipulus Vocabulorum*. This 'Handful of Vocables' was the first attempt at an English dictionary of rhymes. The contents are arranged in accordance with their terminations. The book has nine parts, divided according to the nine vowels that occur before the consonant in the last syllable of the word listed. The total of nine vowels is obtained by adding to the five simple vowels, *a, e, i, o, u*, the diphthongs, *ay, ea, oy, ou*. Accent marks are found in this dictionary, at those places 'where the sillable must go vp & be long'.

One of the quaintest of all the early dictionaries was *An Alvearie or Triple Dictionarie, in Englishe, Latin, and French*, published in 1573 by John Baret or Barrett, a Fellow of Trinity College, Cambridge. How his dictionary was made and how its unusual name originated he tells in his address to the reader:

About eyghteene yeares agone, hauing pupils at Cambridge studious of the Latin tongue, I vsed them often to write epistles and themes togither, and daily to translate some peece of English into Latin, for the more speedy, and easie attaining of the same. And after we had a little begunne, perceyuing what great trouble it was to come running to mee for euery word they missed, (knowing then of no other Dictionarie to helpe vs, but Sir Thomas Eliots Librarie, which was come out a little before) I appoynted them certaine leaues of the same booke euery day to write the English before ye Latin, and likewise to gather a number of fine phrases out of Cicero, Terence, Cæsar, Liuie, &c. and to set them vnder seuerall Tytles, for the more ready finding them againe at their neede. Thus within a yeare or two they had gathered togither a great volume, which (for the apt similitude betweene the good scholers and diligent Bees in gathering their wax and hony into their Hiue) I called then their Aluearie, both for a memoriall by whom it was made, and also by this name to incourage other to the like diligence, for that they should not see their worthy prayse for the same, vnworthily drowned in obliuion.

This brief notice of a few of the sixteenth-century dictionaries is sufficient to show that the chief motive underlying lexicography up to 1600 was to assist students of foreign languages, Latin, French, Italian, Spanish. Apparently it did not occur to any one before the close of the sixteenth century that there was need for a dictionary altogether in English which would help English people to understand their own language. The need for dictionaries altogether in English arose in a rather interesting way.

We have already called attention to the fact that the English language at all stages of its existence has added to its vocabulary by borrowing from other languages. William Caxton was entirely correct in saying that so far as their use of language was concerned Englishmen seemed to be born under the domination of the ever-changing moon. For a long time the taking over by English of terms from other languages excited little or no comment, but before Caxton's death in 1491 mutterings of protest were beginning to be heard.

The purists began to voice their objections to the new terms coming into English. In 1532 Berthelette brought out an edition of the *Confessio Amantis* in which he commended the 'worthy olde wryter John Gower' for having used 'englysche words and vulgars'. Sir Thomas Elyot congratulated himself upon the fact that Henry VIII upon reading the *Governour* 'perceyued that through out the boke there was no terme new made by me of a latine or frenche worde, but it is there declared so playnly by one mene or other to a diligent reder, that no sentence is therby made derke or harde to be vnderstande'.

The following excerpts from the Preface of Andrew Boorde's *Dyetary* (1547 ed.) furnish good examples of the kind of writing that failed to meet with the approval of those who advocated the use of pure English:

To the armypotent Prynce and valyent lorde Thomas Duke of Northfolke Andrewe Boorde of physycke doctor: dothe surrender humyle commendacyon with immortall thankes.

After the tyme that I had trauelled for to haue the notycyon & practes of Physycke in diuers regyons & countres. . . .

The mesage done, I with festynacyon & dylygence dyd nat prolonge the tyme. . . .

The which dyd know, nat onely your complexcion & infyrmite, but also . . . the imbecyllyte and strength of your body, with other qualytes expedyent & necessary to be knowen: but brefely to conclude, [for] your recuperatyng or recouering your health . . . [I] was compocated [*sic*] to be in the presence of his magesty. . . .

I . . . hauyng a cotydyal remembrance vpon youre bountyfull goodnes, dyd consulte with many egregyous Doctours of physycke . . . for the conseruacyon of the health of youre body. . . .

And where I haue dedycated this boke to your grace, And haue nat ornated hit with eloquence & retorycke termes, the whiche in all maner of bokes and wryttynges is vsed these modernall dayes, I do submytte me to your bountefull goodnes.

With such specimens as these from Boorde before us, it is easy to understand how Wilson could write in his *Art of Rhetoric* (1553):

Some seke so farre for outla*n*dishe Englishe, that thei forget altogether their mothers la*n*guage. And I dare swere this, if some of their mothers were aliue, thei were not able to tell, what thei say, & yet these fine Englishe clerkes, wil saie thei speake in their mother tongue, if a ma*n* should charge the*m* for cou*n*terfeityng the kynges English. Some farre iorneid ientleme*n* at their returne home, like as thei loue to go in forrein apparell, so thei wil pouder their talke wt ouersea la*n*guage. He that cometh lately out of France, wil talke Frenche English, & neuer blushe at the matter.

Sir John Cheke, the famous Greek scholar, took sides with those who believed that English 'should be written cleane and pure'. Sir John feared that the continual borrowing from other languages would cause English to keep 'her house as bankrupt'. Gascoigne in his *Certayne Notes of Instruction* (1575), warned his reader against thrusting into verse words of many syllables. Gascoigne was enough of a philologist to know that as a rule 'the most auncient English wordes are of one sillable'.

Angel Day in *The English Secretorie* (1586), commented upon and objected to the use of such words as *egregious*, *eximious*, *vrbanitie*, *exasperate*, *insipient*, *inarcious*, *arcane*, &c. Nash and Harvey during the inky war which they carried on with each other toward the close of the sixteenth century quarrelled about words and expressions like 'conscious mind', 'canicular tales', 'egregious argument', 'putative artists', 'rascallitie', 'materiallitie', &c.

On the other hand, there were numerous defenders of the taking over into English of such terms as were in dispute. Richard Eden regarded English as having been enriched by its numerous borrowings from Latin, and he proposed to continue this borrowing. George Pettie's opinion of the taking of Latin words into English may be found in the introductory part of his translation of Guazzo's *Ciuile Conuersation* (1586 ed.):

For the barbarousnesse of our tongue, I must likewise saie that it is much the worse for them [traducers of England], and some such curious fellowes as they are: who if one chance to deriue anie word from the Latine, which is insolent to their eares (as perchance they will take that phrase to be) they forthwith make a iest at it, and tearme it an Inkhorne tearme. And though for my part I vse those wordes as little as anie, yet I know no reason why I should not vse them, and I finde it a fault in my selfe that I doe not vse them: for it is in deed the readie waie to inrich our tongue, and make it copious, and it is the waie which all tongues haue taken to inrich themselves. . . . I meruaile how our English tongue hath crackt it credit, that it may not borrow of the Latine as wel as other tongues: and if it haue broken, it is but of late, for it is not vnknowen to all men, how many wordes we haue fetcht from thence within these few yeeres, which if they should be all counted inkpot tearmes, I know not how we should speak anie thing without blacking our mouths with inke: for what word can be more plain than this word (plaine) & yet what can come more neere to the Latine? What more manifest than (manifest)? & yet in a manner Latine.

Writers who did not share Pettie's liberal sentiments regarding language made an effort to restore to use archaic words. The works of writers like Chaucer and Trevisa were ransacked for words. So many difficult words, many of them archaic, appeared in English of the sixteenth century that glosses were made for some of the works of that time. Possibly the best known are those which E. K. added to Spenser's *Shepheardes Calender* of 1579. The appearance of these glosses in the first edition of the *Calender* is significant as showing that such aids were felt to be necessary at the time the work was first published.

III

FROM CAWDREY TO JOHNSON

THE sixteenth-century agitation over 'inkpot' and 'inkhorn' terms did not prevent foreign words of all kinds from pouring into English. These borrowings came from actual contact with the people of other countries, and from the increasingly numerous books on many subjects that were being printed. The need of the time was clearly for dictionaries altogether in English which would enable English people to understand their own language.

Robert Cawdrey was the first to supply his countrymen with an English dictionary dealing with the hard words that had become common in the language. His *Table Alphabetical* appeared in 1604. In his preface Cawdrey gave his readers the following instructions, which in this day of scientific pedagogy may be worth repeating:

> If thou be desirous . . . rightly and readily to vnderstand, and to profit by this Table, and such like, then thou must learne the Alphabet, to wit, the order of the Letters as they stand, perfectly without booke, and where euery Letter standeth: as (b) neere the beginning, (n) about the middest, and (t) toward the end.

Cawdrey's dictionary was quite small, containing approximately three thousand words. A slightly larger work of the same kind appeared in 1616. This was Dr. John Bullokar's *English Expositor: Teaching The Interpretation of the hardest words vsed in our Language*. The *Expositor* was very popular and appeared in successive editions for more than a hundred years following its first appearance, a thirteenth edition being brought out at Dublin in 1726. In a third edition published in 1663 at London, Bullokar added an index of 'ordinary English' words defined in terms of a more 'scholastick' nature. *Bashful* had *Verecund* as its corresponding learned equivalent; *Howling* was the same as *Ululation*; *Huckster* the same as *Regrator*, &c. A third division of the book was a 'brief Nomenclator' of the 'most memorable Things and famous Persons'. Stray bits of curious information were scattered through Bullokar's dictionary. For example, under *Beaver* in the main vocabulary the author explained that a beaver coming into a strange colony was immediately pounced upon by the resident beavers, who reduced him to the status of a slave, pulling out the hair from his back so that he could easily be recognized as an interloper.

Another noticeable feature of these early dictionaries that were devoted to the explanation of hard words is the absence from them of many words which the modern reader would expect to find included. For example, in the third edition of Bullokar the words *arcane, conservacyon, convocated, cotydyal, inarcious, ornated, retorycke,* are not found. On the other hand, many of the words that do appear in this and earlier editions—words like *citation, civic, clandestine, clemency*—are now accepted as quite commonplace.

The first work to have the title of *The English Dictionary* was produced in 1623 by Henry Cockeram, Gentleman. Like many others of its time, it was *An Interpreter of hard English Words*. The little volume was divided into three parts. Part I was devoted to the 'choisest words themselues now in vse, wherewith our language is inriched and become so copious'. In this part occur among many more common terms, such words as:

Abecedarian, One that teacheth the Crosse-row.
Abequitate, To ride away.
Bubulcitate, to cry like a cow boy.
Sulleuation, a murderous intent.

Part II gave the explanation of 'vulgar' words in terms

of greater difficulty, a reversal of the process used in Part I. The following are typical entries:

Baked. *Pistated.*
to Banquet. *Obligure.*
to Bolt a doore. *Obserate.*

Part III treated of 'Gods and Goddesses, Men and Women, Boyes and Maides, Giants and Diuels, Birds and Beasts, Monsters and Serpents, Wells and Riuers, Hearbs, Stones, Trees, Dogges, Fishes, and the like'. In this part of the work one reads that a crocodile is 'a beast hatched of an egge, yet some of them grow to a great bignesse, as 10. 20. or 30. foot in length: it hath cruell teeth and scaly back, with very sharpe clawes on his feete: if it see a man afraid of him, it will eagerly pursue him, but on the contrary, if he be assaulted he wil shun him. Hauing eaten the body of a man, it will weepe ouer the head, but in fine eate the head also: thence came the Prouerb, he shed Crocodile teares, *viz.* fayned teares'.

In 1656 Thomas Blount, a barrister of the Inner Temple, published his *Glossographia*. In his introduction he explained that while bestowing 'the waste hours of some years in reading our best English Histories and Authors' he was often 'gravelled' by such words as *Janizaries, Seraglio's, Urim*, &c. He had also observed many new words, like *Piazza, Balcone, Rochet, Capouch*, making their appearance among various classes of society. Inspired by the presence in the language of much that he could not readily understand, he devoted the 'vacancy of above Twenty years' to compiling his dictionary, which was 'intended for the more-knowing Women, and less-knowing Men; or indeed for all such of the unlearned, who can but finde in an Alphabet, the word they understand not'. Blount's little volume possessed some notable features. In it are found crude efforts at etymology. Most of the words are referred to the languages from which they come, and frequently the source word in the foreign language is given, as Cognition (*cognitio*), Mastication (*masticatio*). Blount also cited authors or works as authorities for some of the words he included. The Bible and legal statutes were cited most frequently. In at least two places, in connexion with the heraldic terms *canton* and *gyron*, Blount used illustrations of a shield to help out his definitions.

The *Glossographia* was in 1658 used by Edward Phillips, nephew of John Milton, as the basis of his *New World of Words*. In the fourth edition (1678) there is a section devoted to 'such affected words from the *Latin* or *Greek*, as are either to be used warily, and upon occasion only, or totally to be rejected as Barbarous, and illegally compounded and derived'. Among these barbarous words are a few expressions now quite respectable, for example:

To *Agonize*, (Greek) to play the Champion or valiant Combatant.
Bibliography, (Greek) a writing Books.
To *Evangelize*, (Greek) to write or preach the Gospel.
Ferocious, (Lat.) fierce or cruel.

Blount did not relish having his work plagiarized, but he restrained himself until Phillips brought out a law dictionary, which Blount regarded as another theft from a work of his called *Nomolexicon*. Feeling that patience had ceased to be a virtue, Blount in 1673 published

A world of errors discovered in the New World of Words, or General English Dictionary; and in Nomothetes, or the Interpreter of Law-Words and Terms.

In this work Blount doubtless over-estimated the injury he had received at the hands of Phillips, but some of his *notes* are rather racy:

Bigamy, the marriage of two Wives at the same time, which according to Common Law hinders a man from taking holy orders.

Here our Author speaks some truth, at peradventure: For he that marries two Wives at the same time commits Felony, and the punishment of Felony is Death; which (suppose it be by hanging) may very well hinder him from taking holy Orders—I find he does not understand the word.
Gallon (*Spanish*), *a measure containing two quarts*. Our Author had better omitted this word, since every Alewife can contradict him.

Works concerned primarily with the explanations of hard words survived into the eighteenth century. John Kersey, an unusually energetic worker, after bringing out in 1706 a revision of Phillips's *New World of Words*, published his own *Dictionarium Anglo-Britannicum*, in 1708. This dictionary was devoted to the 'explication' of hard words, including such as Kersey had searched for in various English dialects, and in numerous old records, charters, and statutes. He placed all the words he dealt with in one vocabulary, and indicated the sources of many of them by appropriate abbreviations. *Leethwake*, meaning pliable, limber, and *Nittle*, handy, neat, are examples of dialect words found in Kersey's work; while *Rymmers about* ('Vagabonds, or idle roaming Fellows'), and *Titinylk* ('a Tale-bearer'), are representative words collected from old records. Chatterton is said to have obtained many of his archaic terms from Kersey's pages.

It is perhaps not generally known that John Wesley, the father of Methodism, is entitled to a place among English lexicographers. His little dictionary came out in 1753, and bore on its title-page some quaint information:

The Complete English Dictionary, Explaining most of those Hard Words which are found in the best English Writers. By a Lover of Good English and Common Sense. N.B. The Author assures you, he thinks this is the best English Dictionary in the World.

In addition to the works that we have just enumerated,

all of them following in the Cawdrey 'hard word' tradition, there were in the seventeenth century dictionaries in which etymology was given a place. This feature, as we have noticed, appeared in Blount's *Glossographia*, but the idea was not original with Blount. Etymology was given some attention in the most monumental and laborious lexicographic work of the seventeenth century, which was John Minsheu's *'Ηγεμὼν εἰς τὰς γλώσσας, id est, Ductor in Linguas*. This Guide into the Tongues published in 1617, was a polyglot dictionary in eleven languages, English, British or Welsh, Low Dutch, High Dutch, French, Italian, Spanish, Portuguese, Latin, Greek, Hebrew. Minsheu was a teacher of languages, and, as one might guess, was poor in the goods of this world; yet in the preparation of his *Guide* he managed to employ a number of scholars, both native and foreign. By this means he 'runne himselfe into many and great debtes, vnpossible for him euer to pay....' It is in Minsheu that we have the choice derivation of the term Cockney:

A COCKNEY or COCKNY, applied only to one borne within the sound of Bow-bell, that is, within the City of London, which tearme came first out of this tale: That a Cittizens sonne riding with his father out of London into the Country, and being a nouice and meerely ignorant how corne or cattell increased, asked, when he heard a horse neigh, what the horse did; his father answered, the horse doth neigh; riding farther he heard a cocke crow, and said doth the cocke neigh too? and therfore *Cockney* or *Cocknie*, by inuersion thus: *incock*, q. *incoctus*, i. raw or vnripe in Country-mens affaires. But in these daies we may leaue the terme *Cockney*, and call them *Apricockes* or *Abricockes*, in Lat. *præcocia*, i. *præmatura*, i. soone or rathe ripe, for the suddainnesse of their wits, whereof commeth our English word *Princockes*, for a ripe headed yoonge boie....

Minsheu's dictionary is credited with being the first book published by subscription in England. It was a work memorable for having made some effort to arrive at the etymology of words and for citing authors' names, and occasionally passages from their works, in the treatment of some of the words.

In 1671 there was published posthumously the *Etymologicon Linguæ Anglicanæ* of Dr. Stephen Skinner (1623–67). This was, from the standpoint of etymology at least, the most notable contribution to lexicography made in the seventeenth century. The vocabulary was a five-fold one. The first was composed of ordinary words, the second of botanical terms, the third of forensic terms, the fourth of Old English words, and the fifth of proper names, including names of rivers, regions, cities, towns, mountains, &c.

Later in the century, in 1689, appeared an anonymously written dictionary called the *Gazophylacium Anglicanum.* It contained some amusing etymologies. In his preface the unknown author says, 'The chief reason why I busied myself herein, was to save my time from being worse employed.'

In 1743, sixty-six years after the death of its compiler, Francis Junius (1589–1677), appeared the *Etymologicum Anglicanum.* This work was a great aid to Johnson, and has been called 'the first systematic and comprehensive work on the analogies of our tongue'.

It must of course be borne in mind that the etymologies given in early dictionaries were often more curious and interesting than genuinely instructive. As examples of the more absurd etymologies found in seventeenth-century dictionaries the following from the *Gazophylacium* of 1689 will serve, although even that work cannot fairly be judged from these exceptionally poor examples:

Hazle-nut, from the AS. Haesl-nutu, the Belg. Hasel-noot, or the Teut. Hasel-nuʒ, the same; all perhaps from our word *haste*; because it is ripe before wall nuts and chestnuts.

Hassock, from the Teut. Hase, an hare, and Socks; because hair-skins are sometimes wore instead of socks, to keep the feet warm in winter.

The seventeenth century was prolific in types of dictionaries. During the century bilingual dictionaries continued to be brought out. In 1677 Elisha Coles, teacher of Latin and student of shorthand, brought out his dictionary of English-Latin and Latin-English, a work which enjoyed great popularity and within a century passed through many editions. Coles is also remembered in connexion with a preface he wrote for a dictionary of hard words which he produced in 1676. In this preface he made some sharp criticisms of his predecessors in the field of lexicography, and cited such entries as the following to show the ignorance displayed in some dictionaries:

Lungis, a tall slim Man that has no length to his height,
Mayweed, like Cammomile in smell, but of a stinking savour,
Nazareth, the place where Christ was born.

In discussing the *Dictionarium* of 1708 we made mention of the fact that Kersey included in this work some dialect words. Thirty-four years earlier, however, John Ray had produced a work which he called *A Collection of English Words not Generally used, with their Significations and Original, in two Alphabetical Catalogues, The One of such as are proper to the Northern, the other to the Southern Counties.* This work turned out to be far more popular than Ray had expected. People from various parts of England sent him additional local terms which he was pleased to acknowledge and make use of in an enlarged second edition in 1691. We shall see that at a later date the study of English dialects was carried on with great thoroughness. John Ray may fairly be given credit for being a pioneer in paying attention systematically to the various dialectal peculiarities. Professor Skeat said that he was, 'after a manner, the remote originator of the English Dialect Society'.

We have already called attention briefly to Elisha Coles and his dictionary of 1676. In this dictionary Coles included some slang terms, justifying himself by saying in his preface: ''Tis no disparagement to understand the Canting Terms: it may chance to save your throat from being cut, or, at least, your pocket from being pickt.' As Coles indicated, slang had its beginnings in the speech of beggars, vagabonds, and gypsies. Long before Coles's time attention had been given to the language of the canting crew. As early as 1561 John Awdelay, a printer-author, wrote a small work called *The Fraternitye of Vacabondes*. Though Awdelay's book was not a dictionary of cant language, it contained a great many terms belonging to the vocabulary of beggars and thieves. Awdelay's explanations of these terms are interesting. For example, '*Esen Droppers* bene they, that stand vnder mens wales or windowes, or in any other place, to heare the secretes of a mans house. These misdeming knaues wyl stand in corners to here if they be euill spoken of, or waite a shrewd turne.'

It is not necessary to enumerate the many works dealing with the activities and language of thieves which quickly followed Awdelay's work. Toward the end of the seventeenth century there appeared *A New Dictionary of the Terms Ancient and Modern of the Canting Crew, in its several Tribes, of Gypsies, Beggers, Thieves, Cheats, &c.* The author of this work did not care to have his name known in connexion with it. As a result the book is said on the title-page to be written 'By B. E. Gent'. The unknown author explains in his preface that some terms of 'Quality and Fashion' are in his dictionary, and many of the expressions included are not and never were slang. At the same time, there do occur a fairly large number of expressions, the respectability of which is not yet established, and the antiquity of which might not be suspected. For example, *Fence* is given as the term for 'a Receiver and Securer of Stolen-goods'; *Flush in the Pocket*, 'full of Money'; *Half Seas over*, 'almost Drunk'; *Hick* . . . 'silly Country Fellow', &c.

Interest in slang continued during the eighteenth century. Francis Grose in 1785 produced a slang dictionary, to which he gave the paradoxical title *A Classical Dictionary of the Vulgar Tongue.* A reference to Grose's *Classical Dictionary* is apt to mislead one who does not know that it is a dictionary of slang. Some of the entries in this work are amusing, as may be seen from the following treatment of Gouge, a 'vulgar' Americanism that is now no longer needed:

Gouge, to squeeze out a man's eye with the thumb, a cruel practice used by the Bostonians in America.

No doubt many people in thinking about dictionaries regard them as books whose function it is, among other things, to include *all* the words in a language. There is not, and probably never will be, any dictionary containing all the words in the English language. It was not until the eighteenth century that an English dictionary made any effort to include all words, the common ones as well as the hard terms.

In 1702 there appeared *A New English Dictionary; or, a compleat collection of the most proper and significant words, commonly used in the language*. . . . The author of this work signed himself J. K., and has quite naturally been identified as John Kersey, a lexicographer whom we have already met. No matter who the author was, his dictionary, as we can tell from its title, marked a new departure in lexicography. Attention was henceforth to be given to that part of the vocabulary which was most used.

In 1721 Nathan Bailey published his *Universal Etymological English Dictionary: comprehending the Derivations of the Generality of Words in the English Tongue, either Antient or Modern.* Bailey's dictionary was a distinct improvement on its predecessors because (*a*) it was more comprehensive in scope, (*b*) it laid increasing emphasis on etymology, (*c*) it gave in the edition of 1731 aid, though of an elementary sort, in syllabification and pronunciation. Other features of the work were the inclusion of illustrations in a fuller supplementary volume of 1727, and the introduction of proverbs and current sayings. Accent marks were also used in this 1727 volume. In 1730 Bailey brought out a folio volume entitled: *Dictionarium Britannicum: Or a more Compleat Universal Etymological English Dictionary Than any extant.* A second edition appeared in 1736. This *Dictionarium* was an important work. It was an interleaved copy of this folio dictionary which Samuel Johnson used as a basis of his dictionary. Bailey was easily the most important lexicographer before Johnson.

In the first half of the eighteenth century there was a very decided tendency toward 'correcting and purifying' language. France and Italy had established Academies, the chief objects of which were to improve and establish permanently the modern languages. Swift and others recommended an Academy for England, but no such institution was established. The Italian and French Academies had in the seventeenth century produced dictionaries, the Italian work coming out in 1612, the French in 1694. Various people in England, among them Dodsley the publisher, Alexander Pope, Warburton, and Samuel Johnson, were thinking about the compilation of a new English dictionary based upon the usage of recognized authorities. Pope drew up a list of writers whose works should be examined for the dictionary. In some way this list came into the possession of Samuel Johnson, who entered into a contract with several London publishers to prepare a dictionary for £1,575. Johnson believed that he could complete the dictionary in about three years, but in this idea he was mistaken.

Johnson took up his quarters in a house which is still pointed out in Gough Square, just off Fleet Street, in London, and began toiling away at his herculean task. Sir John Hawkins gives the following account of how he carried on his work:

Johnson, who before this time, together with his wife, had lived in obscurity, lodging at different houses in the courts and alleys in and about the Strand and Fleet street, had, for the purpose of carrying on this arduous work, and being near the printers employed in it, taken a handsome house in Gough square, and fitted up a room in it with desks and other accommodations for amanuenses, who [*sic*], to the number of five or six, he kept constantly under his eye. An interleaved copy of Bailey's dictionary in folio he made the repository of the several articles, and these he collected by incessant reading the best authors in our language, in the practice whereof, his method was to score with a black-lead pencil the words by him selected, and give them over to his assistants to insert in their places. The books he used for this purpose were what he had in his own collection, a copious but a miserably ragged one, and all such as he could borrow; which latter, if ever they came back to those that lent them, were so defaced as to be scarce worth owning, and yet, some of his friends were glad to receive and entertain them as curiosities.

During the time he was at work upon his dictionary Johnson was also engaged in other enterprises. It was nearly seven years before he could make the following entry in his diary:

Apr. 3, 1753. I began the second vol. of my Dictionary, room being left in the first for Preface, Grammar, and History, none of them yet begun.

Two years later, on April 15, 1755, the completed work in two volumes was placed on the market.

The most commendable features of Johnson's dictionary were the full treatment of the various senses of words, and the extent to which standard authors were drawn upon for quotation to illustrate these meanings. In his use of authorities Johnson did not cite writers prior to the sixteenth century, public opinion in his day being that in the seventeenth and early eighteenth century the language had reached the high-water mark of its perfection. Unfortunately Johnson did not date his quotations, and in many instances did not give the title of the works from which they were taken, contenting himself with ascribing them to Dryden, Prior, &c. The amount of reading which Johnson did for his dictionary was prodigious. In his two volumes there are extracts from several hundred prose writers and poets. Johnson's definitions were, as a rule, improvements upon those given by previous lexicographers.

For the century after the first appearance of Johnson's dictionary that work dominated the field of English lexicography. It went through many editions and revisions, and was drawn upon freely by practically all of Johnson's successors. The only advance which the eighteenth century made over Johnson's lexicographic methods was in orthoepy, or pronunciation. Bailey (1727) had used accent marks, and Johnson had marked accented syllables, but it was not until the appearance of Dr. William Kenrick's *A New Dictionary* in 1773 that much help was given for pronouncing all the syllables of a word. Kenrick marked the separate syllables with a number referring to a table of English sounds. He omitted a large number of words the pronunciation of which was difficult or doubtful.

Thomas Sheridan, an elocutionist, after having worked twenty years on a system of English pronunciation, brought out in 1780 *A General Dictionary of the English*

Language. Sheridan, though an Irishman, felt himself capable of grappling with the difficult question of English pronunciation, since he had a schoolmaster who was the intimate friend of Swift and of many other literary men of Swift's time. For several months Sheridan read to this master three or four hours every day and received in a full measure the benefits of his corrections in pronunciation. Despite Sheridan's confidence in his ability, his pronunciations came in for severe criticisms, one critic going so far as to say that he had produced a work which was more 'a national disgrace than ornament'. One thing criticized was his making *-ciation* a disyllable instead of a trisyllable. For example, *renunciation* was to be pronounced re-nun-sha-shun.

The most famous name in connexion with pronunciation in the eighteenth century is that of John Walker, an actor and elocutionist, whose dictionary came out in 1791. This work passed through many editions at the hands of numerous revisers, and was for a hundred years regarded both in England and in America as the chief authority on pronunciation. John Pickering, of whom we shall have more to say later, on page 42 of his *Vocabulary* of 1816, noted with satisfaction 'a general and increasing disposition' on the part of the American people to regulate their pronunciation by that of Walker. It is interesting to examine an early edition of Walker and to notice with what care he commented on pronunciations. Here, for example, is the comment on *Garden*:

> When the *a* in this and similar words is preceded by G or K, polite speakers interpose a sound like the consonant *y* which coalesces with both, and gives a mellowness to the sound. thus *a Garden* pronounced in this manner is nearly similar to the two words *Egg* and *Yarden* united into *eggyarden*, and *a Guard* is almost like *eggyard*.

This peculiarity of pronunciation is still met with in some

places in the United States, especially in parts of Virginia. The pronunciation *goold* for *gold* which James Fenimore Cooper recommended to his countrymen was not endorsed by Walker, though he recorded the fact that *goold* had for some unaccountable reason come to be more used than *gold*, the proper pronunciation.

In the latter part of the eighteenth century lexicographers adopted the device of placing stress marks in such a way as to terminate syllables and thereby aid in the pronunciations of words. The Rev. John Ash in his *New and Complete Dictionary of the English Language*, of 1775, took credit upon himself for having used stress marks in this manner. Entries in his dictionary like *Ab'bacy*, *Art'ful*, *Ar'tery*, show the helpfulness of his arrangement. In his introduction Ash said he had included in his dictionary 'all the words he could find or remember'. In his efforts to find words he examined closely earlier dictionaries. His use of Johnson's dictionary caused him to make a very amusing mistake about the etymology of the word *curmudgeon*. The origin of this word is unknown, but in Johnson's dictionary of 1755 he made use of a suggestion given him by an unknown correspondent who thought that *curmudgeon* came from *cœur méchant*, the French for 'evil heart'. Johnson's etymological note on the word was, 'It is a vitious manner of pronouncing *cœur mechant*. Fr. an unknown correspondent.' Ash completely misunderstood Johnson and in his dictionary derived *curmudgeon* '*from the* French cœur, *unknown, and* mechant, *a correspondent*.'

By way of summary, we may notice that the 'hard word' tradition in dictionary making persisted for a century and a half after the publication of Cawdrey's *Table* in 1604. As early as 1674 John Ray interested himself in dialectal expressions, and at about the same time Elisha Coles admitted into his dictionary (1676) some slang expressions of a sort that had earlier interested John Awdelay and others. Thomas Blount, in his *Glossographia* of 1656, tried his skill at etymology. In the eighteenth century common words began to engage the attention of lexicographers. Johnson's dictionary, based on the idea of standardizing the language, and with well-chosen quotations from standard authors to illustrate the definitions, which in themselves were much better than those previously given, came out in 1755. Towards the close of the eighteenth century great advances in orthoepy were made by Kenrick, Sheridan, and Walker. To the eighteenth century may also be assigned the beginnings of the inclusion in dictionaries of synonyms, an improvement introduced in 1774 by the Rev. James Barclay in his *Complete and Universal English Dictionary*.

IV

THE NINETEENTH CENTURY

At the opening of the nineteenth century lexicography was in the hands of revisers and supplement makers. No one questioned the supremacy of Johnson and Walker, or aspired to do more than amend the works produced by them.

George Mason in 1801 brought out a work which he frankly entitled *A Supplement to Johnson's English Dictionary*. Mason continued Johnson's plan of exemplifying the meanings of words by means of extracts, and asserted in his preface that he had been much more particular in his references than Johnson had been. But an examination of the *Supplement* shows very little more exactness in references than Johnson had used. Mason possibly congratulated himself on having more consistently than Johnson referred to specific works.

The Rev. Henry J. Todd was another nineteenth-century reviser of Johnson, his work appearing in 1818. Todd devoted himself mainly to improving Johnson's etymologies, and to adding words which Johnson had not included. Todd brought the vocabulary of Johnson's dictionary up to approximately 58,000 words. This was a larger number of entries than had previously been placed in a dictionary. In the following year, 1819, another minister, the Rev. John Seager, brought out a supplement to Johnson.

Still another lexicographer who aspired to supplement Johnson was Richard P. Jodrell whose *Philology on the English Language* appeared in 1820. In his preface Jodrell said he had 'sacrificed three years and an half' of his 'advanced life' to this work. He estimated that approximately 17,520 terms were dealt with in his volume. The entries in his dictionary were placed in the centre of the column, instead of being brought back flush with the left-hand margin. Jodrell felt that this arrangement might become popular, but it has not done so. The words supplied by Jodrell, additional to those contained in Johnson, show a preponderance of comfortable, mouth-filling words and combinations printed as single words. Expressions like *courserbreeding, courtbutterfly, masterconscience, mountainminer, pistolbullet, womanglutton,* are examples. *Phantomnation,* one of Jodrell's combinations, deceived some later dictionary makers, who regarded it as a formation with the suffix *-ation,* and recorded it as such in their dictionaries.

In 1847 there appeared volume I of a work bearing the title *A New Universal Etymological, Technological, and Pronouncing Dictionary of the English Language.* This volume had no preface or foreword of any sort, but on the page following the title there was a

Notice.

This Work will be finished in Two Volumes. On its completion the Author will doff his anonymous position, and appear in his proper character . . . he humbly trusts, to his own credit, and to the satisfaction of his numerous and respectable patrons.

The next year volume II appeared and bore on its title-page the name of John Craig. In the preface to this volume Craig explained that he had planned to compile a universal dictionary based on those of Johnson and Walker. He expressed his appreciation of Webster's dictionary, which, he pointed out, was the first English dictionary possessing at once etymological, technical, and pronouncing features. But because Webster had not done as well as he might have in dealing with pronunciation or with the natural sciences, Craig felt disposed to offer his own work as an improvement. Craig's praise of Webster shows the coming into recognition of the New England schoolmaster who became one of the foremost lexicographers of his day, and an interrupter of the Johnsonian tradition in dictionary making.

In discussing Webster's contribution to lexicography it is well to bear in mind that during the last part of the eighteenth century there was among the Atlantic colonists a rapidly growing feeling of Americanism. The citizens of the colonies were coming to regard themselves as chosen inhabitants of a goodly land. It was felt that the noblest institutions of civilization would reach in North America a fullness of perfection that had never been achieved elsewhere. How this attitude of confidence in the country's high destiny influenced the thoughts of some patriots regarding the future of the English language in this new environment may be seen from the following extract from page 6 of *The Royal American Magazine* for January, 1774. The writer signed himself 'An American', but his further identity is not known:

And as Language, is the foundation of science, and medium of communication among mankind, it demands our first attention, and ought to be cultivated with the greatest assiduity in every seminary of learning. The English language has been greatly improved in Britain within a century, but its highest perfection, with every other branch of human knowledge, is perhaps reserved for this Land of light and freedom. As the people through this extensive country will speak English, their advantages for polishing their language will be great, and vastly superior to what the people in England ever enjoyed. . . .

On September 5, 1780, John Adams, who later became second President of the United States, addressed an eight hundred word letter to the President of Congress suggesting the high perfection to which the English language would come in this country, and advising that Congress consider the 'erecting' of an 'American Academy for refining, improving, and ascertaining the English Language'. The results of the Revolution were of course highly gratifying to loyal Americans and increased their feeling of present and destined superiority in all realms of human activity.

Noah Webster (1758–1843), more than many of his contemporaries, shared in this enthusiasm for his native land. In 1783 he published what after many revisions became his famous *Elementary Spelling Book*, the old 'Blue Backed Speller', and acting on the advice of Dr. Goodrich, a trustee of Yale, he kept up his lexicographical interests. In 1806 appeared his

> Compendious Dictionary of the English Language. In which FIVE THOUSAND Words are added to the number found in the BEST ENGLISH COMPENDS, The ORTHOGRAPHY is, in some instances, corrected; The PRONUNCIATION marked by an Accent or other suitable Directions; And the DEFINITIONS of many Words amended and improved. To which are added for the benefit of the MERCHANT, the STUDENT and the TRAVELLER, I.—TABLES of the MONEYS of most of the commercial Nations in the world, with the value expressed in Sterling and Cents. II.—TABLES of WEIGHTS and MEASURES, ancient and modern, with the proportion between the several weights used in the principal cities of Europe. III.—The DIVISIONS of TIME among the Jews, Greeks and Romans, with a Table exhibiting the Roman manner of dating. IV.—An official List of the POST-OFFICES in the UNITED STATES, with the States and Counties in which they are respectively situated, and the distance of each from the seat of Government. V.—The NUMBER of INHABITANTS in the United States, with the amount of EXPORTS. IV. [*sic*]—New and interesting CHRONOLOGICAL TABLES of remarkable Events and Discoveries.

A glance at this title-page shows that the work possessed a large amount of encyclopedic material that has no connexion with lexicography. At the opening of the nineteenth century libraries and books of reference were scarce in this new land, and people were poor. Webster made an effort to give his patrons as much as he possibly could for their money. This encyclopedic feature is one which has especially characterized American dictionaries, though it is not a distinctively American innovation.

Regarding the changes he had introduced in his dictionary Webster wrote in his preface:

> No great changes should ever be made at once, nor should any change be made which violates established principles, creates great inconvenience, or obliterates the radicals of the language. But gradual changes to accommodate the written to the spoken language, when they occasion none of these evils, and especially when they purify words from corruptions, improve the regular analogies of a language and illustrate etymology, are not only proper, but indispensable.

When Webster brought out this first dictionary, he had not delved very deeply into the study of language, and had not developed those eccentricities which later marked his views of philology. In his dictionary of 1806, however, there were some features which to a greater or less extent characterized his later dictionaries.

One of these features had to do with spelling. Webster regarded the English dictionary makers as having in some instances adopted spellings which were needlessly different from those in use at an earlier time. That dictionary makers and grammarians are great corrupters of language was a conviction which Webster reached early in his career. Many of the spellings which he adopted in his 1806 dictionary were simplifications arrived at by omitting silent letters, for example, *favor, honor, savior; logic, music, physic; cat-cal, etiquet, farewel, foretel; ax, disciplin, examin, libertin; benum, crum, thum* (verb). Other simplifications were made in the interests of analogy, for example, *ake, checker* (for chequer), *kalender, skreen; croop, soop, troop; fether, lether, wether; cloke, mold, wo; spunge, tun, tung.*

Words in *-re* were spelled by Webster with the *-er* termination, and he justified this ending by the example of such writers as Newton, Camden, Milton, Selden.

Just as errors had crept into orthography, so had faulty pronunciations come about by a failure on the part of dictionary makers and grammarians to discover that 'ease of pronunciation and the melody of sounds' were leading principles governing pronunciation.

In his treatment of the content of the vocabulary Webster showed his independence in two ways. He left out of his 1806 dictionary such words as *daggledtail, decumbiture, depasture, deuteroscopy*. These omissions, however, may not have been wilful, as he included these words in his 1828 work. His feeling was that a dictionary should not include such useless expressions. On the other hand, he included words the respectability of which was at that time questioned. Some of these were *appreciate*, in its sense of to 'rise in value', *applicant*, 'one who makes request', *advocate*, as a verb, *Congressional, Departmental, lengthy, Presidential.*

Another feature of Webster's first dictionary was the distinction made in it between American and English usage. These distinctions were not at all numerous, but there were enough of them to attract the unfavourable notice of some of the critics of the work.

So numerous and severe were the criticisms of this first dictionary that in 1809 Webster wrote two letters to a friend of his, the Hon. Thomas Dawes, explaining at some length why he considered his critics unfair. His answer to the criticism that he had included localisms in his work was that every lexicographer had done the same. In proof he cited Johnson as having put in his dictionary such localisms as *hog*, meaning sheep, and *tup*, meaning ram. He admitted that he had included some cant words like *caucus*, but pointed out that he had purged the vocabulary of other words like *fishefy, jacalent, jiggumbob.* To make up for this deletion, he asserted that he had enriched the vocabulary by including a great many words like *accompaniment, adjutancy, advisory, amendable, animalize, ascertainable, insubordination, subsidize.*

While carrying on an inky war with his critics and expending an amazing amount of energy in a dozen different directions, Webster was hard at work on a much more elaborate dictionary. He spent nearly twenty years on the new project. It was his custom to rise about half an hour before the sun, 'and make use of all the light of that luminary'. He remarks, 'While engaged in composing my Dictionary, I was often so much excited by the discoveries I made, that my pulse, whose ordinary action is scarcely 60 beats to the minute, was accelerated to 80 or 85'. He did not in his work receive any encouragement worth speaking of, either from his countrymen or from foreign scholars. His criticisms of Johnson and his somewhat eccentric pronouncements on the subject of language and grammar had injured his popularity at home and abroad. As he went on with his work he found that there did not exist in America resources such as he needed in the completion of his task. Accordingly, in 1824, he went to Europe, first to Paris and next to Cambridge, England. At Cambridge he completed his great undertaking. 'When I finished my copy,' he wrote afterwards, 'I was sitting at my table in Cambridge, England, January 1825. When I arrived at the last word, I was seized with a tremor that made it difficult to proceed. I, however, summoned up strength to finish the work, and then walking about the room I soon recovered.'

In 1828, when Webster was seventy years old, his large dictionary came out in two volumes. It contained about 70,000 entries, or about 12,000 more than Todd's revision of Johnson (1818). The size of Webster's vocabulary was augmented by the inclusion of many words like *deathful, death'sdoor, death'sman, dewlapt*, the omission of which in his 1806 dictionary had distressed one of his Boston critics. But he resolutely kept out *fishefy, jacalent*, and *jiggumbob*. The title of his second dictionary, *An American Dictionary of the English Language*, reflected Webster's conviction that the time had arrived for an *American* dictionary, 'for', as he said in his preface, 'although the body of the language is the same as in England, and it is desirable to perpetuate that sameness, yet some differences must exist'. He cited such expressions as *land-office, land-warrant, location of land, regent* of a university, as examples. In his preface also he expressed the pride which he felt in being able to cite as authorities Franklin, Washington, Adams, Jay, Madison, Marshall, together with Boyle, Hooker, Milton, and Dryden. Webster brought out a revision of his large dictionary in 1840. He was at work upon a further revision at the time of his death in 1843.

It is not easy to sum up briefly the influence which Webster exerted upon orthography in the United States and upon lexicography. Through his *Spelling Book* and his dictionaries he reached millions of people. We have noticed the esteem in which John Craig held Webster, but Craig's judgement was by no means that of all Webster's contemporaries. During his long and busy life Webster had voiced many interesting but unsound views on the subject of language. He wounded the sensibilities of a large number of people, who found it more pleasant to familiarize themselves with his eccentric utterances than to read what he had actually placed in his dictionary. The result was that Webster was disliked by a number of people.

Webster's *American Dictionary*, considered in the light of its time, was a notable contribution to lexicography, but its shortcomings were many. The etymologies were in many instances quite wrong. The starting-point of

Webster's deficiency in etymology was his full acceptance of the Mosaic account of the dispersion of the human race. The theory of one parent speech existing in the land of the Chaldees being accepted, he reasoned out 'affinities' in languages with no regard at all to actual facts or to geography. All he needed was some suggestion of physical resemblance in the words themselves, and he was able to attend to the details needed to establish kinship. For example, *Diana,* the name of the goddess of the chase, suggested the Celtic word *dian,* meaning 'swift', 'eager', 'strong', and Webster immediately saw an 'affinity'. Yet far more of Webster's etymologies were correct than those of any lexicographer who had preceded him. He made many mistakes, but he got many things right.

Space need not, of course, be taken here to comment in detail upon Webster's theories of orthography, and upon the changes which he advocated. Any just view of his ideas about spelling must take into account the fearful hodge-podge which English presents in that respect, and yet modern spelling appears regular and orderly when compared with that which was used in earlier times. One can get some conception of the possibilities of English spelling at an early date by remembering that even for proper names variant spellings existed in profusion. Thomas Fuller was told that the name *Villiers* is spelled fourteen different ways in the family records. The name of Shakespeare's father appears in sixteen different spellings. The family name Mainwaring is said to have been spelled in one hundred and thirty-one different ways. Efforts to introduce some order and regularity into English spelling began as far back as the early part of the thirteenth century when Orm wrote his *Ormulum.* From that time to the present day there have been scores of people who have struggled with schemes for reducing English spelling to some semblance of reasonableness. Noah Webster was merely one of these strugglers, and his efforts, viewed in comparison with others made before and during his time, appear very sane and commendable.

Briefly, the changes in spelling advocated by Webster were based on (1) the etymology of the words concerned, and (2) analogy with similar words. Of the changes made in the 1828 dictionary on the basis of etymology, many were dropped by Webster himself in his 1840 edition. *Gimblet, iland, nusance, wo,* were some of the words placed back in their commonly found forms. But the changes made in the interests of analogy or uniformity, he more consistently retained, and in the case of some words American and English usage to-day follows Webster's lead. For example, we no longer write *proveable* along with *approval*, or *bedawb* by the side of *daub*. Such changes as Webster made affected a fairly large number of very common words, the frequent occurrence of which tended to magnify the importance of the alterations.

In Webster's large dictionaries of 1828 and 1840 appears little indication of pronunciation. In the introduction of the 1828 work he wrote at length on pronunciation, criticizing Sheridan and Walker quite freely, but saying that some of the finer points in pronunciation could not be put down on paper. Only occasionally did he rewrite a word to show its pronunciation, and his diacritical marks were few and not very exact.

Webster was not the first American to compile a dictionary. Samuel Johnson, Jr. (1757–1836), a native of Connecticut, brought out a small dictionary about 1798. Johnson later collaborated with the Rev. John Elliott, a direct descendant of the John Eliot who was a missionary to the Indians, in producing another small dictionary. Caleb Alexander (1755–1828), also a New Englander, brought out his *Columbian Dictionary* in 1800. But all of these dictionaries were small, and possess little interest beyond that which is inevitably attached to 'firsts' of anything.

While Webster was busily engaged upon his 1828 dictionary there appeared two other American dictionaries, both of them of minor importance. In 1813 Richard S. Coxe, a Princeton graduate, published at Burlington, New Jersey, his *New Critical Pronouncing Dictionary of the English Language.* This work was based on Johnson and Walker and possessed little distinctive interest. Two years later the Rev. Burgiss Allison published, likewise at Burlington, *The American Standard of Orthography and Pronunciation.* This was an abridged dictionary for use in schools. In compiling it Allison had excluded such 'unchaste', 'low', or 'indelicate' expressions as were not appropriate for youth. In preparing this work Allison was evidently associated with a large number of helpers whose 'next design' was 'to furnish the publick with the *American Standard* in a common octavo, without abridgment'. The name of John Pickering appears in the list of those interested in this project for an unabridged *American Standard.* The work itself never appeared.

More nearly on a par with Webster's work is that of Joseph Emerson Worcester (1784–1865), who, after having been engaged upon dictionary projects of many kinds, brought out a dictionary of his own in 1830. Two years before he had prepared an edition of Johnson's dictionary, and in 1829 he had made an abridgment of Webster's *American Dictionary.* His own dictionary of 1830, entitled *A Comprehensive Pronouncing and Explanatory Dictionary of the English Language,* passed through various editions. He continued his work in lexicography and in 1846 produced *A Universal and Critical Dictionary of the English Language.* A pirated edition of this was brought out in London and advertised as being 'compiled from the materials of Noah Webster, LL.D., by Joseph E. Worcester'.

Finally, as an improved and enlarged edition of his work, Dr. Worcester completed in 1860 *A Dictionary of the English Language*, in one volume. This contained about 104,000 entries, a larger number than any other dictionary at that time contained. Synonyms were given some attention, and for improving this feature Worcester may fairly be given credit. Illustrations also were used, a fact that has caused some writers to ascribe to Worcester the honour of first having employed this device, but illustrations had been used in dictionaries before.

The personal unpopularity of Webster did a great deal to advance for a time the popularity of the Worcester series of dictionaries. Many people were quick to resent Webster's criticisms of the learned Samuel Johnson, and to judge the New Haven schoolmaster's dictionary in the light of Webster's numerous eccentricities. Worcester was conservative in orthography and pronunciation and had a calmer outlook upon his work than had Webster. By advertising himself as desirous of recording the language as it actually was, without trying to change or improve it, Worcester emphasized the feeling held by some people that Webster was a rank iconoclast, a 'critick and coxcomb general of the United States'. In July 1860, the faculty of the University of Virginia formally went on record as favouring the use in their institution of Worcester's Dictionary 'as the standard of propriety'. Commenting on the word *bub*, Holmes in the first chapter of *The Poet at the Breakfast Table* (1872), playfully hints at the popularity in Boston of Worcester's dictionary, 'on which, as is well known, the literary men of this metropolis are by special statute allowed to be sworn in place of the Bible'.

Webster's death caused his somewhat trying personality to recede in importance in any consideration of the successive editions of the dictionary, and the growing popularity of the dictionaries bearing his name prevented the

Worcester series from attaining as wide a circulation as it might otherwise have had. Though the edition of 1860 was reprinted many times and augmented by a Supplement, no modern revision of Worcester's large dictionary has been made.

In the middle of the nineteenth century John Ogilvie brought out his *Imperial Dictionary, English, Technological, and Scientific; Adapted to the Present State of Literature, Science, and Art; on the Basis of Webster's English Dictionary.* This work of Ogilvie's, published in 1850, in two large handsome volumes, is noteworthy because (1) in it are clearly seen traces of the encyclopedic features which were to be further exploited in subsequent works, and (2) Ogilvie in his preface called attention to the fact that in dictionary making the United States was at that time in advance of England. In this preface he wrote, 'Webster's dictionary which forms the basis of the present work, is acknowledged both in this country and in America to be not only superior to either of the two former [Johnson and Richardson], but to every other dictionary hitherto published'. The best-known edition of Ogilvie's dictionary is that of 1881–3, edited by Dr. Charles Annandale.

Robert Gordon Latham, a native of Lincolnshire, brought out his *Dictionary of the English Language* in 1866–70. Latham, although he based his dictionary on Todd's edition of Johnson, did a great deal of independent reading, especially of nineteenth-century authors, and thus secured many quotations, with references, for his dictionary. His work was drawn upon largely by later dictionary makers.

We have already called attention briefly to the fact that Ogilvie's *Imperial Dictionary* possessed encyclopedic features. Ogilvie wrote, 'The *Imperial Dictionary* will be found to contain, along with the etymologies and the definitions of words and terms, a large amount of useful and interesting information connected with literature, art, and science'. Ogilvie included such information 'so that the charge usually preferred against English dictionaries, namely, that they furnish but *dry sort of reading*, will not apply to this dictionary'. As an example of the sort of information which Ogilvie felt justified in giving, the following taken from the entry *Bustard* will serve: 'This fowl grows to the weight of twenty-five or twenty-seven pounds, with a breadth of wing of six or seven feet. It inhabits England, feeding on green corn and other vegetables, and on earth-worms. It runs fast and takes flight with difficulty.'

This practice of including in a dictionary information which would more logically be found in an encyclopedia became popular. It was a pronounced feature of a seven volume (or fourteen 'divisional' volume) work which came out from 1879 to 1888, with a supplementary volume in 1902. This was frankly called the *Encyclopædic Dictionary*. Sometimes it is referred to as *Cassell's Dictionary*, having been published originally by Cassell, Petter, Galpin & Co. In 1895 the same work was published by the firm of Edward Lloyd, Limited, and was consequently called *Lloyd's Encyclopædic Dictionary*. This dictionary was republished many times, both in England and in America. It has appeared with various titles, such as *The Imperial Dictionary*, *The People's Dictionary*, *The International Encyclopedic Dictionary*, &c. By whatever name it is known, the work was a very creditable one. The generous attention paid to scientific and technical terms and the care taken to explain the *things* indicated by the entries, added greatly to its value. Pictures and drawings were used freely, especially in connexion with the scientific terminology employed.

The encyclopedic tradition was very definitely carried on in America by the Century Publishing Company which began in 1882 to prepare its well-known publication, *The Century Dictionary, An Encyclopedic Lexicon of the English Language.* This work was edited by William Dwight Whitney, Professor of Comparative Philology at Yale University. The first three volumes, comprising *A* to *L*, were published in 1889, volumes iv and v, advancing the work as far as *Stro-*, appeared in the following year, and in 1891 the work was completed with volume vi. *The Century Cyclopedia of Names* was added in 1894, and *The Century Atlas of the World* in 1897. A Supplement in two volumes came out in 1909. The most recent edition, that of 1911, contains twelve volumes, the first ten being taken up with the vocabulary, and the eleventh and twelfth being respectively *The Cyclopedia of Names* and the *Atlas*. In its most modern form the *Century* contains over 500,000 entries, being by far the most elaborate lexicographic work ever brought out in America. A noticeable and highly commendable feature is its plan of making a main entry of each word or term treated, so that derivative words and compounds are easily found. In dealing with the various meanings of words the plan is followed of marking only clear, easily recognizable distinctions. This method makes for conciseness and a simplicity in treatment which the average user of a dictionary appreciates.

In the next dictionary to claim attention, *A Standard Dictionary of the English Language,* the encyclopedic method was followed. This work was published by Funk and Wagnalls Company in 1893–5. Dr. Isaac Kauffman Funk, the editor of the *Standard,* was first a Lutheran minister, and later a journalist and publisher. In 1890 he was interested in founding Funk and Wagnalls, and in the same year he planned and launched *The Literary Digest*. Dr. Funk ascertained that most people consult a dictionary for one or more of three reasons. They wish to learn of a given word its (1) spelling, (2) pronunciation, (3) present meaning. In addition, he thought, a few people might wish to find out the origin of a word. Acting on these convictions, he edited a dictionary in which he reversed some of the usually accepted dictionary technique. In the *Standard* the spelling and pronunciation of the word come first, then the modern meaning, followed by the older meanings. The derivation comes last of all. By reversing the historical order in dealing with meanings, and by placing first those things likely to be most wanted by the user, Dr. Funk produced a dictionary which could be consulted more efficiently than can most works of the kind. In line with this ideal of efficiency in arrangement, the *New Standard* (1913) has all its entries included in a single vocabulary. This method of entry has proven popular.

A new type of dictionary introduced in the nineteenth century by Charles Richardson forms the subject of a later chapter.

V

SPECIAL TYPES OF DICTIONARIES

THE English language has been taken by colonists to many places remote from England. In these distant places the language has undergone changes that have led to the preparation of what may be called dictionaries of Colonial English. North American colonization was the earliest to be undertaken by England, and naturally it was in the United States that the English language first began to exhibit modifications which aroused—and still arouse—extensive comment. When English people first settled in America they soon began to add to their vocabulary words of Indian origin, like *wigwam, tomahawk, wampum.* They also retained some words that had been in common use in England but had become obsolete there.

The natural result of the linguistic processes that went on was that there came a time when differences between American English and British English were easily apparent. During the two years, 1736–7, that John Wesley spent in the United States he noticed and commented upon words which he regarded as distinctively American. For example, he recorded *bluff* as a term which the Americans used to designate 'any highland hanging over a creek or river'. He also defined *swamp* as 'any low, watery place which is covered with trees or canes'. His observations upon these two words were just, for they are typically American terms. If either of them had an existence in England prior to its occurrence in American usage, evidence of such existence is lacking.

The first writer, so far as is now known, who gave much attention to the American English which he heard in use in this country was Jonathan Boucher who came to Virginia in 1759 to act as tutor in the household of a Captain Dixon. Boucher made his home in America until the outbreak of the Revolutionary War. About 1770 he drew up a list of some American words and expressions which he heard used in Virginia and Maryland. Some of the words which he noticed as being distinctive of the country were, *johnny-cake, mush, hominy, pickaninny, samp, yam, loblolly, pone, Manitou.*

Another early commentator on American English was the Rev. John Witherspoon, who came over from Scotland in 1768 and became president of the College of New Jersey, now known as Princeton University. Dr. Witherspoon in 1781 wrote a series of articles in which he commented somewhat at length on words and expressions which he thought were typically American. For such terms as these he coined the word *Americanisms.* He did not cite many exclusively American expressions, but he condemned the use of 'either' where more than two things were involved, and pointed out the omission of 'to be', 'for', and 'as', in such sentences as 'These things were ordered delivered to the army', 'We may hope the assistance of God', 'I do not consider myself equal to the task'. He mentioned *clever* and *mad* as words that had taken on American senses.

During the first years of the nineteenth century there was much criticism by English travellers, reviewers, and other writers, of the low state of the English language in America. Some of these commentators felt that the Americans, having gained their political freedom from England, were determined to press on and obtain further freedom by so corrupting the English language as to render it unintelligible to Englishmen, or by throwing the language overboard altogether and adopting another in its place. The following excerpt from the *Quarterly Review* for January 1814, p. 528, shows the high-water mark of resentment on the part of one critic against such changes as he thought the Americans were making in the language:

> Nor have there been wanting projects among them for getting rid of the English language, not merely by barbarizing it—as when they *progress* a bill, *jeopardize* a ship, *guess* a probability, proceed by *grades*, hold a *caucus*, *conglaciate* a wave, &c. when the President of Yale College talks of a *conflagrative* brand, and President Jefferson of *belittling* the productions of nature—but by abolishing the use of English altogether, and substituting a new language of their own. One person indeed had recommended the adoption of the Hebrew, as being ready made to their hands, and considering the Americans, no doubt, as the 'chosen people' of the new world.

There is, of course, not the slightest probability that any one in America, or elsewhere, actually had any intention of dispensing with English and adopting Hebrew. The first reply of Americans to the charge that they were ruining the language was that they were simply retaining many expressions which the English themselves had at one time used, but which had with them become obsolete. By examining the earlier records of the language Americans had no difficulty in showing the English origin of a large proportion of the expressions for the use of which they had been censured.

John Pickering (1777–1846), an American lawyer and philologist, resided in London from 1799 to 1801 as secretary to Rufus King, Minister to Great Britain. While in London he became aware of his own use of certain expressions which his English associates assured him were not English, but American. Upon his return to America he continued to give his attention to the subject of language, and in 1814 submitted a paper dealing with the state of the English language in America to the Academy of Arts and Sciences in Boston. This paper was published by the Academy the following year. After considerably expanding and altering his original paper and its accompanying list of words, Pickering in 1816 brought out the work as *A Vocabulary, or Collection of Words and Phrases which have been supposed to be peculiar to the United States of America. To which is prefixed an essay on the present state of the English Language in the United States.* The essay is an interesting one and may be read with profit by students of American English. The *Vocabulary* contained about 500 entries, not all of which, as Pickering was easily able to point out, were of American origin. Pickering's comments on the various words are quite readable. As an example of the interesting treatments of words found in his work, the following will serve. It should be read in connexion with the entry from Grose's *Classical Dictionary,* given on p. 27.

Gouging. The following account of this word is given by an English traveller, upon the authority of an American: 'The General informed me, that the mode of fighting in Virginia and the other Southern States, is really of that description, mentioned by preceding travellers, the truth of which many persons have doubted, and some even contradicted. *Gouging,* kicking, and biting are allowed in most of their battles. . . . *Gouging* is performed by twisting the forefinger in a lock of hair, near the temple, and turning the eye out of the socket with the thumb nail, which is suffered to grow long for that purpose.' . . . The practice itself and the name are both unknown in *New England*; and . . . the practice is much less general in the *Southern States* than it has been.

John Russell Bartlett (1805–86), was the next compiler of what he called a *Dictionary of Americanisms, A Glossary of Words and Phrases, Usually Regarded as Peculiar to the United States* (New York, 1848). Bartlett in his introduction explained that, on comparing the words in his collection 'with the provincial and colloquial language of the northern counties of England, a most striking resemblance appeared, not only in the words commonly regarded as peculiar to New England, but in the dialectical pronunciation of certain words, and in the general tone and accent. In fact, it may be said, without exaggeration, that nine-tenths of the colloquial peculiarities of New England are derived directly from Great Britain'.

Bartlett's *Glossary*, containing as it did about 2,000 expressions, was a much more elaborate work than that of Pickering. In Bartlett's day the modern method of carefully arranging and dating citations had not come into vogue, and many of his illustrative passages cannot now be readily verified. He devoted a great deal of time and labour to his study of words. His opportunities for research were good, as he was for a time librarian of the John Carter Brown Library in his native town of Providence, Rhode Island. The successive editions of the *Glossary* in 1859, 1860, 1877, greatly enlarged upon the original. The latest edition contains about 5,000 entries.

In 1859 there was brought out in Philadelphia a *Glossary of Supposed Americanisms*. The author of this little work was Alfred L. Elwyn, a doctor and philanthropist. The first sentence in Elwyn's preface shows the purpose of the *Glossary*: 'This little work was undertaken to show how much there yet remains, in this country, of language and customs directly brought from our remotest ancestry.' Elwyn had no trouble in showing the English origin of the four or five hundred expressions like *darned, duds, gal, keöw* (cow), which he selected for treatment.

A German-American scholar by the name of Maximilian Schele de Vere, a teacher of modern languages in the University of Virginia, published in 1872 his *Americanisms: The English of the New World*. Schele de Vere adopted an unusual method of treatment for the approximately 4,000 words he dealt with. He allocated the various portions of the vocabulary to their different sources and areas. In his first chapter, for example, he dealt with Indian terms. In the following chapter he took up terms brought in by immigrants. To facilitate ready reference he summed up all the words discussed in alphabetical order in his index. By using this plan he made his book readable, and even entertaining.

The next compiler of a book of Americanisms was an Englishman, John S. Farmer, whose *Americanisms Old and New* was published in London in 1889, being, Farmer said, the first work of its kind ever published on the eastern side of the Atlantic. In his preface Farmer said that the growing prevalence in English usage of Americanisms induced him to produce his work. He was rather given to prophesying, and estimated that within a hundred years the English language would be spoken by 'no less than one thousand millions of people', and he was disturbed at the final result for the language, since, he estimated, the United States would possess by 1900 a population of a hundred millions, 'as against a possible forty to forty-five millions of English subjects'. Farmer made free use of Schele de Vere's work, and cited quite an imposing array of other sources drawn upon. A glance, however, at the long list of 'Authorities and References' placed at the beginning of his volume shows that most of the sources he used were American newspapers of 1888. Despite his diligence, the intricacies of some of the Americanisms he grappled with were too much for him, and the results are sometimes amusing. For example, he explains that the word *jag* 'is also a slang term for an umbrella, possibly from that article being so constantly carried'. He then cites as an illustration the following passage from the *Albany Journal*:

He came in very late (after an unsuccessful effort to unlock the front door with his umbrella) through an unfastened coal hole in the sidewalk. Coming to himself toward daylight, he found himself—spring overcoat, silk hat, JAG and all—stretched out in the bath tub.

Sylva Clapin was the compiler of a volume that appeared in 1902 with the conventional title only slightly varied: *A New Dictionary of Americanisms, being a glossary of words supposed to be peculiar to the United States and the Dominion of Canada.* In his preface Clapin explained that his aim was to produce a book which would appeal to the common reader rather than to the philologist. He proposed to augment preceding works on the same subject by adding terms from the fauna and flora of America, and newspaper and political terms. By his own count Clapin's book contains just 5,258 entries, which are dealt with in the first 424 pages. In the appendices these words are distributed into various groups, and four interesting articles on language are reprinted from English and American periodicals.

The most recent work on Americanisms, that of Richard H. Thornton, may more appropriately be discussed in a later section (p. 69).

The United States was not the only place where Colonial English showed variations from the standards accepted in the mother country. More attention has been paid to Americanisms than to modifications of the language developed elsewhere, largely as a result of the respectable quantity and quality of the literature produced in the United States. Then, too, the early discord which sprang up between England and the American colonists over more vital matters has had a tendency to extend itself in wranglings over differing speech usages in the two countries.

Ever since India and England came into commercial relationship in the days of Queen Elizabeth there have been words of ultimate Indian origin like *calico, chintz, gingham,* making their way by one route or another into the English vocabulary. In 1886 there appeared a collection of these Indian contributions. This work, prepared by Colonel Henry Yule and A. C. Burnell, bore the quaint title *Hobson-Jobson: being A Glossary of Anglo-Indian Colloquial Words and Phrases. . . .* The expression 'Hobson-Jobson' is the British soldiers' version of the cry *Yā Hasan! Yā Hosain!* so often repeated by Mohammedans in their procession of the Moharram in commemoration of the death of Hasan and his brother Hussein. In *Hobson-Jobson* are listed eight or nine thousand expressions, a fairly large number being words like *toddy, veranda, cheroot, nabob, sepoy, shawl, bamboo, pagoda, typhoon, monsoon, mandarin.* A new edition of this interesting dictionary was brought out by William Crooke in 1903.

In 1898 Edward E. Morris, a professor in the University of Melbourne, brought out a dictionary which he entitled *Austral English, A Dictionary of Australasian Words, Phrases and Usages.* Professor Morris in this work calls attention to the fact that the first comers to Australia found a flora and fauna utterly different from anything they had ever known before. 'Since the days when "Adam gave names to all cattle and to the fowl of the air and to every beast of the field" never were so many new names called for.' The exigencies of the situation were met in a way similar to that employed much earlier by the first settlers in North America. Some names were taken over from the aboriginal languages, while others were obtained by attaching new significations to well-known English words. *Boomerang, kangaroo,* and *wombat,* serve as illustrations of words taken over from aboriginal sources; and *wattle,* ordinarily meaning a kind of hurdle, but in Australia applied to a kind of tree the branches of which were excellent for making wattles, represents the second class.

Africanderisms. A Glossary of South African Colloquial Words and Phrases (1913), was the title given to another dictionary of Colonial English. *Africanderisms* was the work of the Rev. Charles Pettman, the scene of whose labours was around Queenstown, South Africa. In an historical sketch at the beginning of this dictionary Pettman called attention to the Dutch, German, French, and English influences traceable in the colloquial South African speech. The vast reaches of Africa have been the meeting places of men from many nations, and the resources of English speech have been augmented by such words as *Kaffir, Bushman, trek, veldt, tsetse, Zulu,* &c.

We have seen in a previous chapter that John Ray directed his attention to dialect words. Others who came after him pursued with great ardour investigations similar in kind to those which he had been interested in. Toward the close of the eighteenth century the Rev. John Jamieson (1759–1838), a native of Glasgow, began to study earnestly the speech of his native land. His interest originated in a discussion with a celebrated scholar who held the view that the speech used in Scotland was not an outgrowth of northern English, but was an independent language, having, like English, its ultimate origin in Gothic. This view, which Jamieson held, is known now to have been quite erroneous, but the work which he performed under the inspiration of his patriotic conception of the independent status of Scottish was of great value. In 1808 he brought out in two handsome volumes his *Etymological Dictionary of the Scottish Language.* This work met with such a favourable reception that in 1818 Dr. Jamieson prepared an abridged edition of it, adding, however, in this a 'variety of words' not found in the original work. So much interest was aroused by these dictionaries that Dr. Jamieson had no difficulty in securing through his own efforts and those of his enthusiastic friends sufficient material for two supplementary volumes, equal in size to the original work. These were brought out in 1825.

At the time of Dr. Jamieson's death in 1838 the results of his labours as a dictionary maker were in an unsatisfactory form. There was the first work in two volumes, produced in 1808, the abridged work of 1818, and the two supplementary volumes of 1825. Because of the fact that the 1818 abridgment contained some words not found in either the 1808 dictionary or the 1825 supplement, the user of Jamieson's work had sometimes to search through three vocabularies before finding the expression he sought. In 1840–1 John Johnstone brought out at Edinburgh a new edition of this dictionary, consisting of two volumes containing in one alphabet the original work of 1808 and abbreviated references to the vocabulary in the Supplement, and two volumes comprising the Supplement itself. The most complete and scholarly edition of Jamieson came out in four large volumes in 1879–82. The editors of this work were John Longmuir, M.A., LL.D., and David Donaldson, F.E.I.S. These editors incorporated the whole of the Supplement with the original work, and also added many words not found in either. They were able also in many cases to improve on Jamieson's etymologies.

The name of Jamieson is easily the foremost one in the field of Scottish lexicography. It was his misfortune, however, to have to carry on his researches at a time when the resources at the disposal of a lexicographer were very inadequate. The texts from which many of his quotations were taken had not been accurately edited, and by depending upon these inaccurate texts Jamieson was sometimes led into errors. Another handicap under which he laboured was the lack of an English dictionary sufficiently comprehensive to enable him to distinguish definitely between English and Scottish.

During the second half of the nineteenth century there was in England a widespread interest in dialect study. How this interest led to the preparation of the *English*

Dialect Dictionary is best told by its editor, Professor Joseph Wright, on page vii of the preface to the first volume, which came out in 1898:

As stated on the title-page, the Dictionary is in a great measure founded upon the publications of the English Dialect Society. It was with this express object in view that the Society was started at Cambridge in 1873, with the Rev. Prof. Skeat as Secretary and the Rev. J. W. Cartmell as Treasurer. In 1876 the Headquarters of the Society were removed to Manchester; when J. H. Nodal, Esq., became the Secretary and G. Milner, Esq., the Treasurer. The Headquarters remained at Manchester until 1893. During these eighteen years Mr. Nodal rendered most valuable services to the Society, and it is not too much to say that it was mainly through his great interest in the subject that the Society published so many excellent County and other glossaries. From 1893 to 1896 the Headquarters were in Oxford, during which time I acted as Secretary and the Rev. A. L. Mayhew as Treasurer. After the Dictionary had been begun, it was no longer necessary to continue the existence of the Society, and it was accordingly brought to an end in 1896 after it had published 80 volumes, all of which are being incorporated in the Dictionary.

In the year 1886 Professor Skeat raised a fund, to which he contributed nearly half the money himself, for the purpose of helping to defray the expenses of collecting and arranging the material for the Dictionary. He had the good fortune to obtain the services of the Rev. A. Smythe Palmer, D.D., who acted as organizing Editor for two years and a half. During this period Dr. Smythe Palmer succeeded in getting together and in arranging in rough alphabetical order a large amount of material. And I take this opportunity of expressing to him my sincere gratitude for all the valuable help he rendered at this initial stage of the work. In 1889 it was thought the material was sufficiently complete to enable me to begin to edit the work for press.'

The sixth and last volume of the *Dialect Dictionary* appeared in 1905. Needless to say, the work is of great usefulness and is without a rival in its own particular field.

The making of slang dictionaries was by no means neglected during the nineteenth century. *A Dictionary of Modern Slang, Cant, and Vulgar Words,* published by John C. Hotten, made its appearance in 1859, and passed through several editions. It was a sizable volume, containing in its later editions 10,000 or more entries. Albert Barrère and Charles G. Leland in 1897 brought out their two-volume *Dictionary of Slang, Jargon & Cant.* This work had been previously issued privately 'for subscribers only' in 1889–90. The most notable work so far done in the field of slang dictionaries appeared in seven volumes from 1890 to 1904. This work, *Slang and its Analogues,* was produced by John S. Farmer, whom we have already mentioned as the author of a work on Americanisms, and W. E. Henley. *Slang and its Analogues* was issued 'for subscribers only', in an edition limited to 750 sets.

VI

THE HISTORICAL PRINCIPLE IN LEXICOGRAPHY

THE major contribution of the nineteenth century to lexicography was the development of the idea of constructing dictionaries on historical principles. In this chapter we shall consider what this idea was and how it was worked out in a practical way.

Charles Richardson (1775–1865) was a man who felt that Johnson and other lexicographers had failed in their dictionaries to take proper account of the ways in which the meanings of a word develop from some one primitive, radical meaning that is shown clearly in the remotest etymology of the word. Preceding lexicographers, so Richardson observed, had contented themselves with giving the meanings, more or less modern, of the words which they recorded, and the immediate, not the remote, sources of the words in English. The result of a procedure of this kind, so Richardson felt, was to ignore in many instances the basic, root meanings of words and to give attention only to late developed meanings and etymologies, some of which completely obscured the remote origins of the words. As an example of Johnson's failure in many instances to exhibit properly the etymologies of words and thus to clear up their earliest meanings Richardson cited Johnson's treatment of the verb *arrive*. Johnson merely referred this word to the French *arriver*, without showing how French had obtained it from Latin or what the force of the Latin expression was. Such etymologizing as this, Richardson thought, did not throw any light on the primitive meaning of *arrive* which Johnson gave, quite correctly, as 'To come to any place by water'.

Richardson's view was that a dictionary should present

such etymologies as would make clear the earliest meanings of words. In his etymology of the word *arrive*, for example, he pointed out that the word goes back to two Latin words which taken together mean 'to the shore'. This etymology gave an explanation of the word's earliest meaning, 'to come to any place by water'. Richardson felt also that sufficient illustrative passages should be utilized in a dictionary to show how derived meanings develop from primitive ones. In 1818 Richardson had an opportunity to begin his lexicographic activities in *The Encyclopædia Metropolitana*, a work brought out in many volumes (1815–45), the early ones being produced under the supervision of Samuel Taylor Coleridge. Richardson's contributions to the *Encyclopædia Metropolitana* furnished the basis of *A New Dictionary of the English Language* brought out in two volumes in 1836–7. In the preface to this dictionary, Richardson explained that in arranging the illustrative quotations in his dictionary he had borne in mind four distinct periods in the history of the English language. The first period, according to Richardson's view, began about 1300 with the works of Robert of Gloucester and Robert of Brunne, and extended to the accession of Elizabeth in 1558. The second period closed with the Restoration of Charles II in 1660, and the third with the coming to the throne of George I, the first Hanoverian king, in 1714. The fourth period extended to the nineteenth century.

Richardson largely dispensed with definitions, numerous quotations from works of the four periods being relied upon to indicate the meanings of the words. He did not date his quotations, no doubt feeling that the intelligent user of the dictionary would know with approximate accuracy the date of such works as Broome, *An Epistle to Mrs. Fenton*: Barrow, vol. iii: J. Philips, *Cider*. The references found in the dictionary were not by any means always explicit. It is a puzzling fact that fuller references were given to citations as they appeared originally in *The Encyclopædia Metropolitana* than in the dictionary.

Both in England and in America Richardson's work obtained wide favour. In completing his preface Richardson wrote, 'At the very moment, when I am concluding this final page, I have reason to believe that the early portions of these volumes have found a resting place upon the tables of an English Settler on the banks of La Pláta: I am assured that they are admitted to relieve the languor of military inaction at the Mess of Abednuggar; and that they have already found employment for the acuteness of nearly a century of critics in the United States of North America.'

The historical method, the general outlines of which Richardson grasped, was followed out logically and completely in the *Oxford English Dictionary*. This great work was the outgrowth of a project of the Philological Society, which was organized in 1842 at London with some two hundred members. The object of the organization was to investigate the structure, affinities, and history of language. In keeping with this purpose the Society in 1857 undertook the collection of such words as had not been included in the dictionaries of Johnson and Richardson. The Committee appointed to have charge of the work issued circulars telling of the Society's plan and inviting the public to help in collecting the words. It was the intention at that time to prepare a supplementary volume, which might be used in connexion with Johnson's or Richardson's dictionary.

The search for unregistered words was so successful that some of the members of the Society felt that it would be wise to extend the project and compile a new dictionary altogether. This view of the matter was strengthened very much by two papers read before the Society on November 5 and 19, 1857, by Dr. Richard C. Trench, at that time Dean of Westminster, and later Archbishop of Dublin. In his papers Dr. Trench dwelt at length upon some deficiencies of the English dictionaries of the time, stressing the fact that there was not in existence a dictionary that gave much information about the history of the words in our language. Without a dictionary on an historical basis it was not possible for any one to know readily the changes in form and meaning which any given word had undergone since its appearance in English. From the dictionaries then in use nobody could find out how long a word had been in the language or which of its many possible senses was the one it had originally, and under what circumstances the word had taken on additional meanings. Dr. Trench further called attention to the fact that many of the older and rarer words in the language had completely escaped the vigilance of Dr. Johnson and his successors. It was recognized that no one man could possibly compass the task of collecting the materials and editing such a dictionary as would take into account the complete life-history of every word that was or had been in the language. Such a work, if done at all, would have to be done by many collaborators working diligently over a period of years and covering the entire range of English literature.

At its meeting of January 7, 1858, the Society resolved to give up the idea of a Supplement and to prepare a new dictionary. The work was placed in the hands of two committees, one literary and historical, the other etymological. Herbert Coleridge (1830–61), great-nephew of Samuel Taylor Coleridge, became the general editor in November 1859, and the work of collecting material went on. Coleridge expended a great deal of time and enthusiasm on the work, but he did not fully realize the magnitude of the task before him and his co-workers. In May 1860 he wrote:

I believe that the scheme is now firmly established, . . . and I confidently expect . . . that in about two years we shall be able to give our first number to the world. Indeed, were it not for the dilatoriness of many contributors, I should not hesitate to name an earlier period.

Coleridge's enthusiasm was contagious, and there was no dearth of volunteers who came forward to help in collecting material. In England there were one hundred and forty-seven who promised to help, and a number of people in America, under the direction of the Hon. G. P. Marsh of Vermont, joined in the work. Coleridge suggested that the Americans make themselves responsible for the reading and extracting to be done from the literature of the eighteenth century, but the suggestion was not seriously taken up.

Rules were drawn up for the guidance of these readers, and a Glossarial Index to the printed literature of the thirteenth century was prepared by Coleridge. The young editor, thinking that one hundred thousand slips would be a sufficiently large number to enable him to begin the actual work of editing the dictionary, prepared lists of words from *A* to *D*, and had some specimen pages containing articles on early words put into type. He devised a set of pigeon-holes that would hold about sixty thousand slips, thinking this contrivance would accommodate the material on which the dictionary would be based. These original pigeon-holes are still to be seen in the Dictionary Room in the Old Ashmolean building in Oxford.

In April 1861, however, Coleridge died, and F. J. Furnivall (1825–1910), succeeded him as editor. Dr. Furnivall realized the great need for more material, and did everything he could to facilitate collecting it. At that time there was a great amount of early English literature that had either never been printed at all or had been very imperfectly printed. For the purpose of rendering this material available in authoritative texts, Dr. Furnivall in 1864 founded the Early English Text Society, which has had a continuous and useful existence to the present day. Four years later he founded the Chaucer Society.

Dr. Furnivall directed readers to 'take one book at least by Fielding, Locke, Defoe, Sterne, Savage, Smollett, Goldsmith, Hogg, Motherwell, Wilson (*Noctes Ambrosianæ*), Sydney Smith, James Mill (*History of India*), Napier (*Peninsular War*), Milman, J. S. Mill, Whewell (*History of Science*), Thackeray, and the host of other writers of whose books none have been yet read'.

In the midst of his numerous activities Dr. Furnivall found time to contribute an amazing amount of material of his own excerpting to the dictionary. From the publications of the societies which he founded and from innumerable other sources, including his morning and evening newspaper, he secured quotations. It was his idea that there should be brought out, as a preliminary to the main work, a 'Concise Dictionary'. He originated the plan of dividing up the material among volunteer helpers who were to arrange the quotations according to senses. For nearly twenty years the energy and ingenuity of Dr. Furnivall and other pioneers in the project were taxed with the many practical problems that had to be dealt with in regard to the preparation of the dictionary. Finally, in January 1879, Dr. Furnivall was able to address the following letter to the members of the Philological Society:

You are aware that for over twenty years the Society has had in hand the preparation of a new English Dictionary, but that from want of funds to pay an Editor to devote a sufficient part of his time to it as his business, and the consequent uncertainty of when the book could be brought out, the work on it has of late years much languisht. But about two years ago, in order to bring the matter to a practical issue, the Council began to negociate with publishing firms, and at last with the Clarendon Press Delegates, with whom they have now settled a Contract, subject to the Society's approval,—to advance money enough to pay an Editor, an assistant, and a couple of clerks, and to undertake the printing and publication of the book.'

Within the next few months the ultimate success of the Society's dictionary project was assured. Dr. James Augustus Henry Murray, the president of the Society, was in 1879 employed as full-time editor of the dictionary, and with him in charge the work went forward persistently. On April 19, 1882, the first copy was ready for the printer, and in November 1883 the first instalment was out of the editor's hands. Dr. Murray continued his work upon the dictionary during the remainder of his life. Through his labours he gained recognition at home and abroad. He became a Fellow of the British Academy, and was honoured with degrees from various universities, including Oxford and Cambridge. In 1908 he was knighted. His great ambition to see the completion of the dictionary by his eightieth birthday was, however, not realized. He died in July 1915.

As the work on the dictionary progressed and as the magnitude of the task became more and more obvious additional editors were secured. Dr. Henry Bradley became connected with the project in 1884, as the result of a brilliant review of the first instalment. He gave assistance with *B* and later began independent editing with *E*. Dr. William A. Craigie was invited to join the dictionary staff in 1897, and four years later began independent editing with the letter *Q*. Dr. C. T. Onions, having joined the staff of the dictionary on Dr. Murray's invitation in 1895, began his work as an independent editor in 1914 with *Su–Sz*. These editors and their helpers carried on their labours at different places. Dr. Murray worked at Mill Hill near London until 1885, when he moved to Oxford. Dr. Bradley at first worked in the British Museum, but in 1896 moved to Oxford and took up quarters in a room at the Clarendon Press. In 1901 the ground floor of the Old Ashmolean in Broad Street, Oxford, was secured for dictionary purposes, and after 1915 the activities of all the staffs were centred there.

Early in 1928, seventy years after the beginning of the undertaking, the Philological Society's project was finished. The completion of the long task was appropriately celebrated on June 6, 1928, at a dinner given by the Prime Warden and Wardens of the Worshipful Company of Goldsmiths. The Goldsmiths' Company had previously, in 1905, contributed £5,000 towards the expenses of publishing the sixth volume of the dictionary. Later in the same month, on June 28, 1928, Dr. Craigie was knighted in token of his achievements in lexicography.

The Philological Society's dictionary has had different titles applied to it. *New English Dictionary*, often abbreviated *N.E.D.* or *NED*, is justified by the title-page of the work itself. For a long time *Notes and Queries* referred to it as the *H.E.D.* (*Historical English Dictionary*). Because Dr. Murray was its original editor the dictionary is sometimes called *Murray's Dictionary*. As early as 1895 the Clarendon Press began to refer to the work as the *Oxford English Dictionary* (*O.E.D.* or *OED*), and this designation is now being used with increasing frequency.

The historical method, followed so completely in the *O.E.D.*, caused scholars to become interested in securing instances of the earliest uses of words. Compilers of dictionaries of a minor range gave dated illustrations of the use of the words they dealt with. Dated quotations are given in the slang dictionary (1890–1904), by Farmer and Henley, and in Morris's *Austral English* (1898), and in Yule and Burnell's *Hobson-Jobson* (1886). A great many dated passages were given by Richard H. Thornton in his *An American Glossary, Being an Attempt to illustrate certain*

Americanisms upon historical principles (two volumes, 1912). This is the most extensive collection of evidence upon Americanisms so far made. The total number of illustrative citations used in the work is about 14,000. Thornton made use of the *O.E.D.* so far as that work was available. He did not cease his collecting of Americanisms with the publication of his *Glossary*. In 1917 he addressed 'an appeal to a large number of wealthy Americans to help the venture financially. To their lasting infamy, they were uniformly too unappreciative to respond'. The additional material was sufficient for a third volume, but the period of the World War was not a time when many people were thinking about the peculiarities of American speech. Thornton entrusted the manuscript of the proposed third volume to Dr. Percy W. Long, at that time Secretary of the American Dialect Society, with the hope that some means of publishing it might be found. So far it has not been practicable to publish the work in book form, but the material is now being printed in special issues of *Dialect Notes*.

The preparation of the *O.E.D.* has contributed to the present conception of the desirability of utilizing its method fully in the making of 'period dictionaries'. The following extract from a paper read before the Philological Society in London in April 1919, by Dr. Craigie, sets forth the whole scheme of Period Dictionaries in an original and authoritative way:

It is recognized by every one who makes use of the Society's Dictionary, that when this work is really finished, it must be followed by a Supplement. . . . When both the main Dictionary and the Supplement are complete, it would be a mistake to suppose that English lexicography has reached its ultimate goal. The Society's Dictionary has easily outstripped anything else of the kind in existence, and contains such a general survey of the English language down to the present day as may never be entirely superseded; but its own plan on the one hand, and the immensity of the material on the other, prevent it from being absolutely final. Dealing as it does with English of all periods, from the 7th century to the 20th, it has been impossible for it (beyond certain limits) to devote special attention to any one of these. Yet each definite period of the language has its own characteristics, which can only be appreciated when it is studied by itself, and which are necessarily obscured when it merely comes in as one link in the long chain of the language as a whole. To deal adequately with each period it is necessary to take it by itself and compile for it a special dictionary, as full and complete as may be. When this process has been completely carried out for all periods, the task of comparison will be a fairly simple one, and it will be easy to see how one differs from another, both in general respects and in special details. As matters stand at present, this can only be done to a very limited extent, with the result that such comparisons as are sometimes made tend to be quite misleading, or at the best are incomplete and unsatisfactory. Without going deeply into details, I may just indicate the nature of the periods which most obviously call for this special treatment:

1. The Old English or Anglo-Saxon period.—This has received a good deal of attention, and now that Prof. Toller's work is finished the vocabulary of Anglo-Saxon is known with a fair approach to completeness. No doubt, in time a revised edition will remove the defects and inconveniences of the present one.

2. The Middle English period, from 1175 to 1500.—The mere vocabulary of this is to a great extent covered by Bradley's edition of Stratmann's dictionary, and for about half of the vocabulary by Mätzner's work. The scale of these, however, makes it quite impossible for them to do justice to this long and varied period, which includes such authors as Chaucer, Langland, Gower, Lydgate, and Caxton. A complete dictionary of Middle English would be a work of marvellous richness and interest, not merely in respect of the language, but for the light it would throw upon the manners and customs of the time. Such a work can never be undertaken on practical

grounds, but in the interests of English Scholarship I hope that by some means or other it may yet be carried out.

3. The Tudor and Stuart period, from *c.* 1500 to 1675.—This is one of the most marvellous periods of the language, and remains almost untouched except in the pages of the Society's Dictionary. Here it bulks very largely indeed, yet by no means more than it deserves. Its riches are almost inexhaustible, and we are almost daily compelled to set aside large quantities of interesting material for which we can find no space in our columns. Moreover, abundant as our material is, it constantly fails to clear up some obscure phrase or allusion, and many well-known passages in the writers of that time still await a satisfactory solution. The English of these two centuries can only be dealt with in an adequate manner when it has been made the subject of special study and has its own dictionary,—a dictionary which would be one of the greatest proofs of the wealth and dignity of the English tongue.

4. The period from *c.* 1675 to 1800 is less remarkable from the purely linguistic point of view, and I am not certain how far it would be worth while to treat it separately from the modern period, which sets in definitely with the 19th century.

5. When we have arrived at the latter date, the problem for the lexicographer is of a different kind. The historic element diminishes, the practical side becomes more prominent. During the 18th century, the scientific terminology had been steadily increasing; in the 19th it assumes overwhelming proportions. Technical language of all kinds, which Johnson was still able for the most part to ignore, pushes its way not only into innumerable special works, but begins to pervade literature as a whole. There is a return to the rich variety of the 16th–17th centuries, made still richer by all the complications of modern conditions. To deal adequately with this demands a dictionary in which there will be little room left for the historical element, because all the available space will be required for the exposition of facts as they are, without regard to what they may have been in the past.

In concluding his address Dr. Craigie laid stress on the

desirability of the preparation of a dictionary of Older Scottish. He pointed out that within recent times a great many of the older Scottish texts and records have been printed for the first time, or in a more correct form than that in which Jamieson knew them, and that this material can now be drawn upon in preparing a dictionary of Scottish as it existed from about 1375 to about 1700.

Since Sir William Craigie submitted his views of Period Dictionaries to the Philological Society considerable interest has been manifested in the preparation of dictionaries along the lines he pointed out.

The Modern Language Association in the United States has taken up the project of compiling a Middle English Dictionary. A few years ago work on the dictionary was begun at Cornell University. Professor C. S. Northup was at that time the editor in charge of the undertaking. At the present time the work is being continued at the University of Michigan with Professor Samuel Moore of that institution as editor.

The University of Michigan has become interested in the proposal for a dictionary of Tudor and Stuart English. Professor C. C. Fries is directing the work on this project.

Sir William Craigie has made substantial progress upon the *Dictionary of the Older Scottish Tongue.* Two parts of the work have already been published.

The Scottish Dialect Committee has undertaken the preparation of a dictionary of Modern Scottish. Dr. William Grant, of Aberdeen, Scotland, is directing this work.

The University of Chicago is sponsoring an historical dictionary of American English. The work being done on this project is under the immediate direction of Sir William Craigie. A large body of material has been brought together at Chicago, and this material is now being put into form suitable for publishing.

The diagram, p. 74, shows the scope of the proposed

Period Dictionaries, and gives some hint as to what is being done upon the various projects.

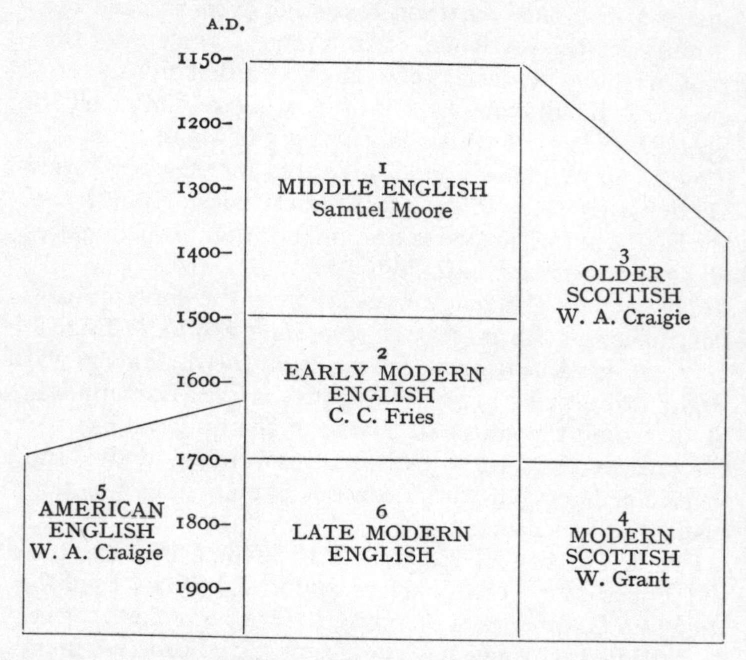

One other dictionary project being undertaken in the United States remains to be mentioned. We have seen that during the latter part of the nineteenth century there was a considerable amount of work done in investigating the various dialects in England and thus laying the foundations for the *English Dialect Dictionary* of Professor Joseph Wright. American scholars felt some of this enthusiasm for dialect study, and as a result they organized at Harvard University in 1889 the *American Dialect Society*. James Russell Lowell and Francis James Child were moving spirits in the formation of this organization. Since 1890 the Society has issued a periodical, *Dialect Notes*, which contains word lists and articles on dialect. So far, more than 30,000 terms have been dealt with in this little publication. It has been the plan of the Society to have its work summed up in a dialect dictionary. In recent years there has been a renewal of interest in the work and aims of the Dialect Society, and hopes have been expressed that at no distant day the actual work of putting the material so far collected, and such other material as should be collected, into permanent form, will be actually begun. Dr. Percy W. Long, who was for many years the Secretary of the American Dialect Society, is the editor of the proposed Dialect Dictionary.

VII

REVIEW OF LEXICOGRAPHIC METHODS

In the preceding chapters we have traced in a very brief manner the general development of English lexicography. Dictionaries, as we have seen, are by no means modern creations, but at the present time they possess features that may fairly be referred to as modern—features that were not even thought of when the first dictionaries appeared.

A good method for (1) showing how dictionaries have become what they are at present, and for (2) indicating the directions in which further developments will have to be made, is to take some common word and show its treatment at the hands of successive lexicographers from very early times to the present. The word *fraternity* is a good one for this purpose. How it has been dealt with in dictionaries from the beginning of the seventeenth century to the present time may be shown as follows.

(1) 1604 Cawdrey

Fraternitie, brotherhood.

(2) 1616 Bullokar

Fraternitie. A brotherhood.

(3) 1658 Phillips

Fraternity (lat.) a brother-hood, also a company of men entered into a firm bond of society, or friendship.

(4) 1754 Martin

Frate'rnity, 1 brotherhood; 2 society, or company.

(5) 1755 Johnson

Frate'rnity, n.s. [*fraternité,* French; *fraternitas,* Latin].

1. The state or quality of a brother.

2. Body of men united; corporation; society; association; brotherhood.

'Tis a necessary rule in alliances, societies, and *fraternities*, and all manner of civil contracts, to have a strict regard to the humour of those we have to do withal. *L'Estrange's Fables.*

3. Men of the same class or character.

With what terms of respect knaves and sots will speak of their own *fraternity*. *South's Sermons.*

(6) 1789 Sheridan

Fraternity, fra[1] tér[1] ni[1] ty[1], s. the state or quality of a brother; body of men united, corporation, society; men of the same class or character.

(7) 1826 Walker

Fraternity, fra[4]-tér[2]-ne[1]-te[1], s. The state or quality of a brother; body of men united, corporation, society; men of the same class or character.

(8) 1828 Webster

Fratern'ity, n. [L. *fraternitas.*] The state or quality of a brother; brotherhood.

2. A body of men associated for their common interest or pleasure; a company; a brotherhood; a society; as the *fraternity* of free masons.

3. Men of the same class, profession, occupation, or character.

With what terms of respect knaves and sots will speak of their own *fraternity*. *South.*

(9) 1836 Richardson

Frate'rnal, Frate'rnity, Frate'rnize, v., Fraterniza'tion, Frate'rnizer. Fr. *Fraternel*; It. *Fraternale*; Sp. *Fraternal*; Lat. *Fraternus*; from *frater*, a brother. The Northern word is probably the root of the Latin: by the literal changes, b, p, ph, f.

To *fraternize*, is a word revived, not created, during the French Revolution. Cotgrave says,

'*Fraternizer,*— to *fraternize*, concur with; be near unto, agree as brothers.'

Fraternal,—of or pertaining to brothers or brethren, to brotherhood; to those united or conjoined as brothers or brethren; brotherly.

With [him] were the templers, & ther *fraternite.*

Fals in alle maners, so tellis the storie me. *R. Brunne,* p. 188.

Thauh he be founde in *fraternite* of all fyve ordres. *Piers Plouhman,* p. 165.

A webbe, a deyer, and a tapiser,
Were alle yclothed in a livere,
Of a solempne and grete *fraternite.*—*Chaucer. Prologue.*

I would be loth to be judged by the only brethren and systers of the false *fraternitie.*—*Sir T. More, Workes,* p. 851.

Thus from the Laureat *fraternity* of Poets, riper years and the ceaseless round of study and reading, led me to the shady spaces of Philosophy; but chiefly to the divine volumes of Plato, and his equal Xenophon. *Id. Apology for Smectymnuus.*

And that M. Furius should ordain a guild, or *fraternitie* out of those that dwelt in the hil of the Capitoll, for the celebration of those plaies.—*Holland. Livivs,* p. 211.

It is also worth our while to consider with what terms of respect and commendation knaves and sots will speak of their own *fraternity.*—South, vol. ii, ser. 6.

Their first charter in which they are styled Peyntours, was granted in the 6th of Edward IV., but they had existed as a *fraternity* long before. *Walpole. Anecdotes of Painting,* vol. i, c. 4.

(10) 1847 Craig

Fraternity, fra-ter′-ne-te, s. (*fraternitas,* Lat.)

The state or quality of a brother; brotherhood; a body of men associated for their common interest or pleasure; a corporation; a company; a society; men of the same class, profession, occupation, or character. In Roman Catholic countries, the word *fraternity* is applied to certain societies which have certain prescribed religious duties and formalities to attend to—as that of the Rosary, who communicate every month, and repeat the rosary continually; of the Scapulary, whom the blessed Virgin, according to the sabbatical bull of Pope John XXII., has promised to deliver out of hell the first Sunday after their death; of St. Francis's Girdle, of St. Austin's Leathern Girdle, &c., &c. The Archfraternity of Charity, instituted by Pope Clement VII., distributes bread every Sunday among the poor, and gives portions to forty poor girls on the feast of St. Jerome, their patron. The Fraternity of Death bury the unclaimed and abandoned dead.

(11) 1860 Worcester

Fra-ter′ ni-ty, *n.* [L. *fraternitas*; It. *fraternita*; Sp. *fraternidad*; Fr. *fraternité*.]

1. State or quality of a brother. *Johnson*.

2. A body of men united for mutual interest or improvement; a society; an association; a brotherhood; as, 'The Masonic *fraternity*'.

3. Men of the same occupation, class, or character. 'The . . . *fraternity* of poets.'—*Milton*.

(12) 1889 *Century Dictionary*

fraternity (fra̤-tėr′ ni̤-ti), *n.*; pl. *fraternities* (-tiz). [⟨ME. *fraternite*, ⟨OF. *fraternite*, F. *fraternité* = Sp. *fraternidad* = Pg. *fraternidade* = It. *fraternità*, ⟨LL. *fraternita(t-)s*, a brotherhood, a fraternity, ⟨L. *fraternus*, brotherly, ⟨*frater* = E. *brother*: see *fraternal*, *friar*, *brother*.] 1. The relationship of a brother; the condition of being a brother or of being brothers; brotherhood. *E. Phillips*, 1706. Hence—2. That mutual interest and affection which is characteristic of the fraternal relation; brotherly regard and sympathy for others, regardless of relationship by blood; brotherhood in general.

For you I have only a comrade's constancy; a fellow-soldier's frankness, fidelity, *fraternity*, if you like; a neophyte's respect and submission to his hierophant; nothing more. *Charlotte Brontë*, Jane Eyre, xxxiv.

The first aspect in which Christianity presented itself to the world was as a declaration of the *fraternity* of men in Christ. *Lecky*, Europ. Morals, ii. 19.

3. A body of men associated by some natural tie, as of common interest or character, of common business or profession, or by some formal tie, as of organization for religious or social purposes; a company; a brotherhood; a society; as, a *fraternity* of monks; a college *fraternity*.

In ye begynnyng it is ordeynede yat yis *fraternite* shal be holden, at ye Chirche of seint Botulphe forsayde, on ye sonday next folowande ye Epiphany of oure lorde. *English Gilds* (E.E.T.S.), p. 15.

With what terms of respect knaves and sots will speak of their own *fraternity*! *South*, Sermons.

Their first charter, in which they are styled Peyntours, was granted in the 6th of Edward IV., but they had existed as a *fraternity* long before. *Walpole*, Anecdotes of Painting, I. iv.

The constitutions of many college *fraternities* are now open to the inspection of faculties; the most vigorous publish detailed accounts of their conventions and social gatherings. *The Century*, xxxvi. 759.

4. Specifically, in the *Rom. Cath. Ch.*, an organization of laymen for pious or charitable purposes, as the special worship of Christ, the honor of the Virgin Mary or of particular saints, the care of the distressed, sick, or dead, etc. Also called *confraternity*, *gild*, or *sodality*. = Syn. 3 and 4. Association, circle, sodality, league, clan.

(13) 1898 *Oxford English Dictionary*

Fraternity (frătə′ɹnĭtĭ). [a. OF. *fraternité*, ad. L. *frāternitāt-em*, f. *frāternus* pertaining to a brother: see Fraternal and -ity.]

1. The relation of a brother or of brothers; brotherhood.

1390 GOWER *Conf.* II. 186 In the virgine, where he [the godhede] nome Oure flesshe and verray man become Of bodely fraternite. 1582 BENTLEY *Mon. Matrones* ii. 22 O my brother what fraternitie! O my child what delectation! 1659 PEARSON *Creed* (1839) 40 If sons, we must be brethren to the only-begotten: but being he came not to do his own will, but the will of him that sent him, he acknowledgeth no fraternity but with such as do the same. 1669 GALE *Crt. Gentiles* I. I. ii. 12 A Phenician Fable touching the Fraternitie of al men made out of the Earth.

2. The state or quality of being fraternal or brotherly; brotherliness.

1470–85 MALORY *Arthur* XVI. iii, Therfor was the round table founden and the Chyualry hath ben at alle tymes soo by the fraternyte whiche was there that she myght not be ouercomen. 1598–9 E. FORDE *Parismus* I. vi. (1636) 34 Those Out-lawes . . continued a great fraternity amongst them. 1605 BACON *Adv.*

Learn. II. To the King § 13 There cannot but be a fraternitie in learning and illumination relating to that Paternitie which is attributed to God. 1793 BURKE *Conduct of Minority* § 35 To substitute the principles of fraternity in the room of that salutary prejudice called our Country. 1844 THIRLWALL *Greece* VIII. 255 It was a treaty of friendship, fraternity, and alliance. 1875 JOWETT *Plato* (ed. 2) III. 106 Equality and fraternity of governors and governed.

†3. A family of brothers. *Obs. rare.*

a 1635 NAUNTON *Fragm. Reg.* (Arb.) 23 When there is an ample fraternity of the bloud Royall, and of the Princes of the Bloud. *Ibid.* 40 Between these two Families, there was . . no great correspondencie . . there was a time when (both these Fraternities being met at Court) there passed a challenge between them.

4. A body or order of men organized for religious or devout purposes.

Letters of fraternity: letters granted by a convent or an order to its benefactors entitling those named in them to a share in the benefits of its prayers and good works.

c 1330 R. BRUNNE *Chron.* (1810) 188 With [þam] were þe templers, & þer fraternite. 1362 LANGL. *P. Pl.* A. VIII. 179 Thauh thou be founden in fraternite a-mong the foure ordres. *c* 1380 WYCLIF *Wks.* (1880) 12 ȝif þei maken wyues and oþer wymmen hure sustris bi lettris of fraternite. 1401 *Pol. Poems* (Rolls) II. 29 Why be ye so hardie to grant by letters of fraternitie to men and women, that they shall have part and merite of all your good deedes? *a* 1512 FABYAN *Will* in *Chron.* Pref. 5 To the fraternytie of our Lady and seynt Anne, w^t^in the said church xii*d.* 1653 H. COGAN tr. *Pinto's Trav.* xxvii. 105 Like unto the fraternity of mercy among the Papists, which onely out of charity . . do tend those that are sick. 1703 MAUNDRELL *Journ. Jerus.* (1732) 70 Each Fraternity have their Altars and Sanctuary. 1788 PRIESTLEY *Lect. Hist.* IV. XXV. 193 In each mitred abbey of the order of St. Benedict, some persons of the fraternity were appointed to register the most considerable events. 1851 D. WILSON *Preh. Ann.* (1863) II. IV. viii. 398 The first recluses and monks who established religious fraternities in Scotland.

5. A body of men associated by some tie or common interest; a company, guild.

c 1386 CHAUCER *Prol.* 364 An Haberdassher and a Carpenter . . clothed in o liveree, Of a solempne and greet fraternitee. 1389 in *Eng. Gilds* (1870) 4 Eche broþer oþer suster þ[t] ben of þe fraternite . . schal ȝeue somwhat in maintenance of þ[e] bretherhede. 1433 *E. E. Wills* (1882) 95 The fraternyte of my crafte of cokes. 1483 CAXTON *Cato* 2, I William Caxton . . of the fraternyte and felauship of the mercerye. 1611 CORYAT *Crudities* 13 This dooth the fraternity of the shoemakers carry in solemne procession. *a* 1674 CLARENDON *Hist. Reb.* xv. § 15 Fraternities enter'd into there for the better carrying on that Plantation. 1762 H. WALPOLE *Vertue's Anecd. Paint.* I. iv. 59 Their first charter in which they are styled Peyntours, was granted in the 6th of Edward IV, but they had existed as a fraternity long before. 1851 D. WILSON *Preh. Ann.* (1863) II. IV. viii. 442 The ancient . . fraternity of Free Masons. 1870 YEATS *Techn. Hist. Comm.* 358 Scarcely a town of importance . . in Italy was without its fraternity of goldsmiths.

attrib. 1671 EVELYN *Diary* 21 Sept., I din'd in the City, at the fraternity feast in yron-mongers Hall.

6. A body of men of the same class, occupation, pursuits, etc.

1561 AWDELAY (*title*), The Fraternitye of Vacabondes. 1653 WALTON *Angler* i. 5 *Auceps.* Why Sir, I pray, of what Fraternity are you, that you are so angry with the poor Otter! *Pisc.* I am . . a Brother of the Angle. 1686 N. COX *Gentl. Recreat.* v. (ed. 3) 44 Some ignorant Grooms . . think they are able to give Laws to all their Fraternity. 1712 HENLEY *Spect.* No. 396 ¶ 2 The Fraternity of the People called Quakers. 1793 BURKE *Conduct of Minority* § 25 The French fraternity in that town. 1838 *Murray's Handbk. N. Germany* 91 Calais is one of those places where the fraternity of couriers have a station. 1858 FROUDE *Hist. Eng.* III. xv. 269 [Henry] was . . ardently anxious to resume his place in the fraternity of European sovereigns.

This list of successive entries possesses some interesting features. The most striking thing about it is the increasing fullness of treatment that characterizes the later dictionaries. Later dictionaries improve upon earlier ones, not only in completeness of treatment, however, but also in accuracy. For example, Johnson (see entry 5 above), in giving the source of *Fraternity* was content to give the Latin word from which it comes, but in the *O.E.D.* (see entry 13), the more exact information is given that the English word is ultimately derived from an oblique case of the Latin word. This gain in accuracy is also noticeable in the use of illustrative citations. A comparison of Johnson's illustrative excerpts with those found in the *O.E.D.* shows quite well the gain in specificness.

Benjamin Martin, whose dictionary is cited in 4 above, was a lexicographer whose work is characterized by the care taken in it to differentiate the various meanings of words. Martin distinguished eighteen 'significations', as he called them, possessed by the verb *set*. The first edition of his dictionary was published in 1749. Entries 6 and 7 show early attempts at indicating pronunciation by using numbers which referred to a table of sounds. Entry 10 shows that Craig's dictionary had some encyclopedic features, though these occur only rarely in it.

A close examination of these specimen treatments shows that a meaning of *Fraternity* quite common in the United States did not attract the attention of lexicographers till comparatively recent times. In *The Century* (see number 12 above), the fact is pointed out that the word sometimes refers to a 'college *fraternity*', and one citation, the date of which is 1888, is given to illustrate that meaning. In later American dictionaries, like the *New Standard* and the *New International*, this meaning receives generous notice. As a matter of fact, the word is used in the United States more often than not to refer to Greek letter societies in colleges and universities. In 1776 the first society of this kind was organized at the College of William and Mary in Virginia. It is clear that from the very beginning the members referred to the organization as a society or as a fraternity, using the two terms quite indifferently, as is shown by recently collected examples of the use of *fraternity* from 1777 onwards.

For three-quarters of a century, however, college men were not very numerous in the United States, and naturally fraternity men were not much in evidence. The result was that *fraternity* in the sense of a Greek letter society, was, generally speaking, confined to a small group, and failed to penetrate thoroughly into common use. In time fraternity men became numerous, the proceedings of their organizations were printed, and the developed sense of *fraternity* finally gained recognition at the hands of lexicographers.

During the years that dictionaries have been evolving into such works as they are to-day, changes have taken place in the methods of compiling them. Unfortunately not much is known about the methods employed by the earliest dictionary makers. We have seen (p. 29) something of the way Johnson set about the task of producing his famous dictionary of 1755.

As a rule, the first step taken in preparing the material for a dictionary is to prepare a 'slip' for each word to be dealt with—a 'slip' being a piece of paper approximately four inches by six inches in size. The kind of information placed on the slip depends upon the purpose and scope of the contemplated dictionary. Nearly all the slips used in preparing a dictionary on historical principles contain the 'catch word', written in the upper left-hand corner, and a passage from some book, newspaper, &c., illustrating the use of the 'catch word'. The source of the passage, the author's name, when known, the date, and the page on which the extract is found are given in some such fashion as shown on the following specimen slips:

Tomahawk, n.

1809 A. Henry, *Travels*, 41.

They walked in single file, each with his tomahawk in one hand, and scalping knife in the other.

Tile-fish, n.

1898 *Boston Record*, 16 Aug. 4/2.

> The U.S. fish commission has located a school of 'tile-fish' off Cape Cod. This valuable food fish was first discovered in 1879. . . . The fish taste like cusk and are very edible. They range from 6 to 50 lb. in weight and can be roughly classed as between channel bass and codfish.

The extract in specimen two is longer than necessary for a dictionary entry, but the entire passage is worth giving because it contains information that may be of use to the editor when he writes the definition of tile-fish.

When a sufficiently large number of slips have been provided and arranged in alphabetical order, the work of editing them may be begun. The slips that contain passages illustrating the same meaning of the word concerned are arranged in the order of their dates and placed together. When this preliminary arrangement has been made for a word in all its meanings, additional slips are prepared, showing the spelling, pronunciation, etymology, and definitions of the word. These slips are then inserted in their proper places.

The editing of a dictionary is work that demands the best care of a capable scholar, but collecting material in slip form can be done by any one with sufficient leisure. Word hunting is an interesting pastime, and the interest which it possesses led hundreds of voluntary readers to supply hundreds and thousands of slips to the editors of the *O.E.D.* for their use in compiling that dictionary.

VIII

CHIEF FEATURES OF SOME MODERN DICTIONARIES

OUR discussion of dictionaries so far has at least suggested the abundance of works of a lexicographic nature that are at present available. It should be remembered, however, that there are literally hundreds of dictionaries of which no account can profitably be taken in a brief treatment like this. There are dictionaries of law, medicine, surgery, theology, chemistry, mineralogy, astronomy, mechanics, commerce, music, &c. Thinking of dictionaries alone, one might to-day voice Solomon's sentiment about the making of many books. The abundance of dictionaries makes it desirable for us in this chapter to call attention to a few of the most outstanding features of some of the best-known modern dictionaries.

At the outset, it should be made clear that there are two features that dictionaries do not possess, although students often assume that they do. Dictionaries do not exclude from their pages such improper words as *ain't* and *hain't*. They frequently record words like these, but they state quite clearly the status which they have in the language. The mere fact that a word is found in the dictionary should not lead one to assume that the word is in good standing. In the second place, dictionaries do not include all the words in the language, even though the tendency is for people to think that they do. A few minutes' reflection will show how impracticable, if not impossible, it would be to include in one dictionary all the words in the language. Such a dictionary, if compiled, would contain such a mass of slang, scientific, technical and trade terms, dialectical and provincial expressions, that the more commonly used part of the vocabulary would be largely submerged. An all-inclusive dictionary would have to contain such slang expressions as *giggle-soup*, *giggle-water*, which are sometimes used in conversation in the United States to mean bootleg liquor. It might even include such a word as *tola*, which has recently been suggested, humorously of course, as a substitute for the longer word *handkerchief*. Such a dictionary would have to provide for monstrosities like *autoawnfeathmattology*, a word made by some dealer in automobile tops, awnings, feathers, and mattresses. Dr. Murray in the General Explanations at the beginning of the first part of the *O.E.D.* wrote with great clarity and wisdom on the scope of a large dictionary. His words are well worth quoting:

The Vocabulary of a widely-diffused and highly cultivated living language is not a fixed quantity circumscribed by definite limits. That vast aggregate of words and phrases which constitutes the Vocabulary of English-speaking men presents, to the mind that endeavours to grasp it as a definite whole, the aspect of one of those nebulous masses familiar to the astronomer, in which a clear and unmistakable nucleus shades off on all sides, through zones of decreasing brightness, to a dim marginal film that seems to end nowhere, but to lose itself imperceptibly in the surrounding darkness. In its constitution it may be compared to one of those natural groups of the zoölogist or botanist, wherein typical species, forming the characteristic nucleus of the order, are linked on every side to other species, in which the typical character is less and less distinctly apparent, till it fades away in an outer fringe of aberrant forms, which merge imperceptibly in various surrounding orders, and whose own position is ambiguous and uncertain. For the convenience of classification, the naturalist may draw the line, which bounds a class or order, outside or inside of a particular form; but Nature has drawn it nowhere. So the English Vocabulary contains a nucleus or central mass of many thousand words whose 'Anglicity' is unquestioned; some of them only literary, some of them only colloquial, the great majority at once literary and colloquial—they are the *Common Words* of the language. But they are linked on every side with other words which are less and less entitled to this appellation, and which pertain ever more and more distinctly to the domain of local dialect, of the slang and cant of 'sets' and classes, of the peculiar technicalities of trades and processes, of the scientific terminology common to all civilized nations, of the actual languages of other lands and peoples. And there is absolutely no defining line in any direction: the circle of the English language has a well-defined centre but no discernible circumference. Yet practical utility has some bounds, and a Dictionary has definite limits: the lexicographer must, like the naturalist, 'draw the line somewhere', in each diverging direction. He must include all the 'Common Words' of literature and conversation, and such of the scientific, technical, slang, dialectal, and foreign words as are passing into common use, and approach the position or standing of 'common words', well knowing that the line which he draws will not satisfy all his critics. For to every man the domain of 'common words' widens out in the direction of his own reading, research, business, provincial or foreign residence, and contracts in the direction with which he has no practical connexion: no one man's English is *all* English. The lexicographer must be satisfied to exhibit the greater part of the vocabulary of *each* one, which will be immensely more than the whole vocabulary of *any* one.

One type of expression likely to be omitted from dictionaries is that represented by such words as *corner-post, corner-tree, fence-corner, fence-post, fence-rail.* There are so many of these combinations in English that no dictionary could possibly include them all. New formations of a similar sort are likely to appear at any time. Most of the large unabridged dictionaries include enough of them to show the possibilities of combinations such as they are. The *O.E.D.* includes more of these expressions than other dictionaries do. Incidentally, the treatment of these in the

O.E.D. directs a student's attention to the fact that English, like German, possesses the ability of increasing its resources by forming compounds. Sometimes German and English are contrasted on the basis of their compound-forming capabilities; German being cited as a language that possesses this feature which English has lost. English has by no means lost this characteristic, though the custom of frequently writing such expressions as *fence rail, fence post*, as two separate words, together with the custom of German dictionary makers of listing under each word its combinations, has had a tendency to divert attention from what are in reality English compounds, and to emphasize German compounds.

Words of recent coinage comprise another group not found fully represented in dictionaries. The words *appendicitis, automobile, pacifist, proton*, for example, could not be included in the *O.E.D.*, as they were unknown at the time the appropriate parts of that work were being compiled. (See Appendix A for the dates of the different parts of the *O.E.D.*) All large general dictionaries have to be constantly augmented by supplements in order to keep up, as nearly as possible, with our ever-growing language. It takes much time and expense to revise unabridged dictionaries. Consequently these dictionaries sometimes do not contain new words that may be found in smaller dictionaries. A dictionary suitable for one's desk, is, as it were, a lighter, faster-moving craft than the ponderous unabridged dictionaries, the battleships, so to speak, of their sort of books. The smaller well-made dictionaries can come nearer keeping up with the words that are new-comers into the language.

Although no dictionary contains all the words in the language, the largest dictionaries present about half a million entries. In such a vast collection of words, the user of a dictionary has to proceed cautiously lest he fail to find the word he is looking for and conclude, erroneously in many instances, that it is not in the dictionary. The larger and more elaborate the dictionary, the more necessary it is that care be used in consulting it. Sometimes competent scholars have, upon consulting some of the larger dictionaries, failed to exercise as much patience and care as they should. An unusual page division in the *New International* makes it necessary for the user of that dictionary to be careful to scan through both the upper and the lower part of the page before giving up a word as missing. Also, the section of 'New Words' that precedes the main vocabulary, has to be examined to make quite sure that the full resources of the *New International* have been utilized.

Another feature of modern dictionaries is the care taken to indicate the pronunciations of the words recorded. The earliest English dictionaries did not give any help with pronunciation, but during the last half of the eighteenth century the compilers of pronouncing dictionaries devised the plan of re-spelling words and placing numbers over the vowels (see p. 77) in the re-spellings to indicate the pronunciations. The numbers over the vowels referred to a list of vowel sounds. Only gradually did the device of re-spelling a word to show its pronunciation make its way into dictionaries other than those devoted to the problems of pronunciation. In Worcester's dictionary of 1860 comparatively few of the words and parts of words were re-spelled for pronunciation. The fact that in English it is necessary to spell a word twice, once to show its proper spelling and again to show its pronunciation, is an impressive comment on the unphonetic character of English spelling.

All modern dictionaries are provided with keys of pronunciation. These keys are different for each of the larger dictionaries, and this lack of similarity in the symbols employed makes it necessary for one who tries to find how a word is pronounced to consult the key in the particular dictionary he is using. The system of keys in which sounds are described by reference to other sounds contained in words that the user of the dictionary is supposed to be able to pronounce correctly is not entirely satisfactory. It is unfortunate that the International Phonetic Alphabet was not devised early enough to be employed, with proper modifications, by the makers of present-day dictionaries. The *Standard* dictionary, when it first came out in 1893, adopted in its re-spellings for pronunciation a scientific alphabet that had been prepared in 1877 by the American Philological Association. It was hoped by the promulgators of this 'Standard Phonetic Alphabet', as it was called, that it would be widely adopted, and its use in such a well-known dictionary as Funk and Wagnalls' was a good recommendation for it. The alphabet, however, did not succeed in winning general approval, and in the course of time it was considerably modified. When the *New Standard* came out in 1913 it made use of the revised phonetic alphabet, and in addition repeated the pronunciations in a system of notation that had long been in use in older dictionaries and text-books. In the *New Standard*, therefore, three spellings are given, the first one to show how the word is spelled, the second to show its pronunciation in the revised scientific alphabet, and the third to show its pronunciation in the older form of phonetic notation. The second re-spelling for pronunciation is apt to be regarded as a second or variant pronunciation, but it is not.

The earliest compilers of pronouncing dictionaries proceeded on the assumption that there was, in practically every case, one, and only one, correct way of pronouncing words, and that it was the proper function of a pronouncing dictionary to set forth these correct ways and thus 'fix' and 'standardize' the pronunciations of the language.

Pronunciations that varied from those endorsed by the makers of these dictionaries were pointed out, usually, only to be censured. The efforts to standardize pronunciation have failed to such an extent that one feature of some modern dictionaries is the attention which they give to recording variant pronunciations. In the *New International* there is a generously long section devoted to showing the pronunciations adopted by some of the leading dictionaries. The plan followed by Dr. Funk, editor of the *Standard*, for showing varieties of pronunciation was an unusual one. He selected prominent scholars and educators in all parts of the English-speaking world to act as an Advisory Committee on disputed spellings and pronunciations. In addition to including the verdicts of this committee on disputed pronunciations, Dr. Funk also indicated in connexion with a number of words pronunciations favoured by various dictionaries and learned societies. A look through that part of the *New Standard* devoted to disputed pronunciations will do much to check any tendency one may have to dogmatize about pronunciations. For the word *adult* four pronunciations are recorded; for *accursed*, six; for *advertisement*, four; for *enunciation*, six; for *typographical*, two, &c.

The spelling of English is more uniform than the pronunciation, but there are many words the spellings of which vary. Some common words like *traveller*, *judgement*, *honour*, *theatre*, *plough*, *mould*, have distinctively British and American spellings. Lexicographers have to take account of different spellings, and they do so in different ways. We have already seen that in the *Standard* recourse was had to an Advisory Committee on spellings and pronunciations. It is interesting to look over the list of words having different spellings in the *Standard* and see how the members of the committee were divided. For example, the spelling *abetter*, was favoured by 24 members of the committee, while 28 endorsed *abettor*. *Jewelry* received the approval of 21 members of the committee; *jewellery* was favoured by 30. *Mood* (the grammatical term) won over *mode* by an endorsement of 47 to 8. Spellings like *favor, honor, labor* won over the fuller forms *favour, honour, labour,* in a ratio of approximately 35 to 18. *Waggon* was favoured by 10 members of the committee.

There has been at different times considerable attention given to the subject of simplified spelling, and there have been prepared lists of words to which the principles of reform spelling were especially applicable. The efforts to simplify English spellings have received only moderate recognition in dictionaries. In the *International* a list of over 3,000 of the proposed simplified spellings was given, but in the *New International* these forms were taken out of the special table in which they had appeared and incorporated as variants in the general vocabulary. Dr. Funk was in sympathy with the movement for simpler spelling, and in the *Standard* he gave space to the reformed spellings, though as a rule the definitions were given only under the usual forms of the words concerned. In the *New Standard* the simplified spellings were retained, but they were entered as variants of the fuller forms. Professor William D. Whitney, a prominent member, and the first president, of the American Philological Association, added as an appendix to the *Century Dictionary* the proposed new spellings. He felt that a more consistent and phonetic spelling was sure to come, and that dictionaries should favour this movement by throwing the weight of their influence on the side of the briefer and more analogical spellings.

We have already seen that from early times dictionaries have possessed encyclopedic features, and we have taken account of the circumstances which induced Noah Webster to provide in his dictionary of 1806 a fairly large body of miscellaneous information that, strictly speaking, has no place in a dictionary. At present a great deal of information of an encyclopedic sort is found in most American dictionaries. The *Century Dictionary*, as we have seen, indicates in its title that it is an encyclopedic work. The *New Standard* is possibly less encyclopedic than either the *New International* or the *Century*, but nevertheless it does contain information that one would expect to find only in an encyclopedia. For example, it records about 65,000 proper names, and among these there are 16,000 personal and biographic entries in the treatment of which recourse was had to encyclopedias and other works of a similar nature. Also, in the definition of some words encyclopedic features are noticeable.

We have seen that the practice of quoting passages from the works of English authors to illustrate the use of words began even before the appearance of Johnson's dictionary in 1755. This practice has continued to the present, and is one of the most noticeable features of all modern unabridged dictionaries. It should be observed, however, that in all modern dictionaries, except the *O.E.D.*, these quotations are used, in the main, to help make the definitions clearer, or to give information about the thing denoted by the entry. They are not used, as they are in the *O.E.D.*, to show the historical development of the different significations of the words under which they are given.

The attention given to synonyms is a characteristic feature of nearly all modern dictionaries. In the *New Standard*, *New International*, and the *Century*, synonyms are given for several thousand words. The *Standard* has antonyms also for a good many of the words whose synonyms are included. This plan of including antonyms was carried over into the *New Standard*, but other dictionaries do not include this feature. In the *Century* homonyms are likewise clearly marked.

The *O.E.D.* is a work that stands apart from all others of a similar sort in that it is a dictionary on historical principles—and the only one in the English language. Many of the features we have discussed as characterizing other dictionaries are not found in the *O.E.D.* No effort is made in it to record a great many variant pronunciations, or to list synonyms, antonyms, homonyms, or to present information usually found in encyclopedias. In the *O.E.D.* there is no biographical or geographical information, or tables of weights and measures, or formulas for ascertaining the day of the week a given date falls upon. The scope of this dictionary was set forth by Dr. Murray in the following words:

> The aim of this Dictionary is to furnish an adequate account of the meaning, origin, and history of English words now in general use, or known to have been in use at any time during the last seven hundred years. It endeavours (1) to show, with regard to each individual word, when, how, in what shape, and with what signification, it became English; what development of form and meaning it has since received; which of its uses have, in the course of time, become obsolete, and which still survive; what new uses have since arisen, by what processes, and when: (2) to illustrate these facts by a series of quotations ranging from the first known occurrence of the word to the latest, or down to the present day; the word being thus made to exhibit its own history and meaning: and (3) to treat the etymology of each word on the basis of historical fact, and in accordance with the methods and results of modern philological science.

Although Dr. Murray and the other scholars associated with him carried on their editorial labours independently, they all kept so steadily in view these aims of the dictionary that no one, from an examination of the completed work, can select the parts done by the different editors.

So much has been written about the *O.E.D.* that it is

not necessary here to do more than to point out a few of the features that are found only in that work.

(1) The various spellings with their approximate dates that words have had through the centuries of their use are exhibited in an abbreviated form just after each entry. The word *yard*, for example, is shown to have had the following forms: ȝeard, ȝerd(e, ȝard(e, yerde, yerd, yaird, ȝherd, ȝord, yorde, ȝharde, yearde, yeard, ȝaird, yarde. As a rule, when one finds an odd-looking spelling anywhere in the whole range of English writings, one has only to turn to the appropriate entry in the *O.E.D.* to find that this particular spelling has been recorded, with an indication of the century or centuries when it was used, and often with an indication of the area in which the form is or was current. It is easy to overlook this unique and valuable feature of the *O.E.D.* To provide that sort of information it was necessary for the editors to have at their disposal a greater wealth of material than any single scholar could possibly have collected.

(2) The etymologies in the *O.E.D.* constitute, probably, its most noteworthy feature. It is not possible for one to appreciate the thoroughness and soundness of this part of that work unless one remembers that what may be called the science of etymology is so young that the common acceptance of its principles has come almost within the lifetime of many scholars now living. Until recent times etymologizing was a pastime that could safely be indulged in by any one who possessed a vigorous imagination and sufficient leisure to speculate about the sources of words. Probably all those scholars who in their prime became sarcastic at the findings of the new school of scientific philologists are now dead, but they have not been dead long.

In fairly modern dictionaries there occur etymologies that are mere speculations that happened to appeal to lexicographers of that time. It used to be a common weakness for philologists to ascribe a word to some little known, far-away source. Another very present help in time of need with earlier scholars was the ease with which one could dismiss a word of obscure origin or doubtful usage by calling it a Scotticism or an Irishism. Speculation about the origin of words has been a popular pastime, and the results are sometimes not as barren of interest as they are of authority. The following, which should be read in connexion with the passage on *Esen Droppers*, p. 26 above, appeared in an American newspaper in 1885, and is typical of much of a similar sort:

> The following account is given of the origin of the term 'eavesdropper'. At the revival of masonry in 1717, a curious punishment was inflicted upon a man who listened at the door of a Masonic meeting in order to hear its secrets. He was summarily sentenced 'to be placed under the eaves of an out-house while it was raining hard till the water ran in under the collar of his coat, and out at his shoes'. The penalty was inflicted on the spot, and the name has continued ever since.

Work on the *O.E.D.* contributed substantially to the extinction of this sort of romantic speculation. For the making of the *O.E.D.* there was brought together literally tons of material illustrating the use of words at all stages of their existence. Never before had the combined resources of so many scholars been utilized for arriving at the origins of English words. Notwithstanding the abundance of material available for the dictionary, there is noticeable in its etymologies a conservatism that is perhaps characteristic of the English people. In places where other lexicographers had been bold enough to bridge the gap between what they knew and what they thought, Dr. Murray and his successors were content to go only as far as the evidence went. They did not fail to point out difficulties in the way of certain explanations about the sources of words. For example, in the treatment of the word *guest*, after pointing out fully the evidence for connecting the modern word with the Old English *ȝiest*, Dr. Bradley, who edited *G*, added a note:

According to phonetic law as at present understood, the initial consonant in the OE. word must have had a palatal pronunciation, which would normally yield ME. ȝ, mod. Eng. *y*. No forms with ȝ or *y* are, however, known to exist; the abnormal guttural pronunciation is usually explained as due to the influence of ON. *gest-r*; but the occurrence of hybrid forms like *gist*, *gust* (ü) in the S.W. dialects of the 13th c. is hard to account for on this supposition.

The Supplement to the *O.E.D.* now being prepared is necessary to take account of the new words that have come into the language, but it is safe to say that so far as the etymological features of the dictionary are concerned no Supplement will ever be necessary.

(3) There is observable in the illustrative excerpts used in the *O.E.D.* a feature that is not characteristic of any other dictionary. In the *O.E.D.* the illustrations are selected in accordance with one prevailing purpose and that is to show the history of the word that is being treated. Other dictionaries that make use of illustrative passages from literature do not include the excerpts for the purpose of showing the history of the words, but rather, as has already been said, with the aim of making the definition clearer or of contributing information about the thing denoted by the word. These motives are worthy ones, but in the *O.E.D.* they give way to the larger purpose for which that work was designed.

Since the historical principle was adhered to so closely in the making of the *O.E.D.* great care was taken to get accurate dates for the passages used and accurate transcripts of them for insertion in the dictionary. Each quoted passage is dated. The date preceding the quotation is that of the composition of the passage, as nearly as could be arrived at. The date, if any, following the name of the author and work cited is that of the edition of the work used to furnish the quotation. The number of illustrative passages included in the *O.E.D.* is nearly two million. No other dictionary of the English language contains more than a fraction of that number.

(4) It has already been pointed out (p. 88) that the *O.E.D.* includes such expressions as *apple-buyer, apple-faced, apple-seller, apple-shaped, apple-wife.* There are so many expressions of this sort dealt with in the *O.E.D.* that one makes no mistake in turning to it first for combinations of this kind. Also, in the *O.E.D.* there is a great deal of information given about the histories of common phrases such as *scot and lot; lock, stock, and barrel; hip and thigh; such carpenters, such chips; Hobson's choice; to walk one's chalks; chip off the old block; up a tree,* &c. Other dictionaries, if they include these phrases at all, do not give much information about their age or origin.

(5) In the *O.E.D.* the differences between British and American usages are in a great many instances carefully pointed out. Attention is also called to the American origin of a great many words like *bogus, gerrymander, hominy, lynch, moose,* &c. Material for tracing the peculiarly American element in the English vocabulary is thus found in the *O.E.D.* To utilize this material fully, however, the student finds it necessary to know which of the works cited in the dictionary are American. Many of the American authors cited, Franklin, Washington, Jefferson, &c., are easy enough to recognize, but there are many others not so well known. In Appendix B (p. 104) there are listed a few of these less well-known American works cited in the *O.E.D.* The list is undoubtedly far from complete, but it may prove helpful. A full record of all the works

read for the dictionary will appear in the Supplement which is now being prepared.

Scholars everywhere have united in paying tribute to the marvellous richness and fullness of information set forth in the *O.E.D.* Those engaged in the editing of writings belonging to any period of English literature find the Philological Society's dictionary indispensable. That work will remain for all time to come a monument to the foresight and zeal of those who conceived it and laid down the generous principles on which it was completed. The making of the dictionary came at an auspicious time. Had the project been undertaken earlier it could not have utilized as it did the findings made in the field of scientific philology. Had the preparation of the work been deferred only a few decades it might not have been undertaken at all, for the diverse and multitudinous ramifications of the English vocabulary, as it has kept pace with human achievements in a great number of fields, might well have cast a damper on the enthusiasm of any who might have aspired to make a complete record of the language

APPENDIX A

The following list shows the parts of the *O.E.D.*, their dates, and how they were combined in the ten volume edition.

Vol. I.	A–Ant	January	1884
	Ant–Batten	November	1885
	Batter–Boz	March	1887
	Bra–Byz	June	1888
Vol. II.	C–Cass	June	1888
	Cast–Clivy	November	1889
	Clo–Consigner	October	1891
	Consig–Crouching	May	1893
	Crouch–Czech	November	1893
Vol. III.	D–Deceit	November	1894
	Deceit–Deject	December	1894
	Deject–Deprav	July	1895
	Deprav–Devel	September	1895
	Devel–Difflu	December	1895
	Difflu–Disburd	June	1896
	Disburd–Disob	September	1896
	Disob–Distrust	December	1896
	Distrust–Doom	March	1897
	Doom–Dziggetai	July	1897
	E–Every	July	1891
	Everybody–Ezod	March	1894
Vol. IV.	F–Fang	November	1894
	Fanged–Fee	April	1895
	Fee–Field	September	1895
	Field–Fish	March	1896
	Fish–Flexuose	September	1896
	Flex–Foister	March	1897
	Foisty–Frankish	October	1897
	Frank–Gain	January	1898
	Gain–German	October	1898
	German–Glasscloth	March	1899

	Glasscoach–Graded	January	1900
	Gradely–Greement	July	1900
	Green–Gyzzarn	December	1900
Vol. V.	H–Haversian	March	1898
	Haversine–Heel	June	1898
	Heel–Hod	December	1898
	Hod–Horiz	March	1899
	Horiz–Hywe	June	1899
	I–In	October	1899
	In–Infer	March	1900
	Infer–Inpushing	July	1900
	Input–Invalid	October	1900
	Invalid–Jew	December	1900
	Jew–Kairine	June	1901
	Kaiser–Kyx	October	1901
Vol. VI.	L–Lap	March	1901
	Lap–Leisurely	January	1902
	Leisureness–Lief	March	1902
	Lief–Lock	January	1903
	Lock–Lyyn	October	1903
	M–Mandragon	October	1904
	Mandragora–Matter	July	1905
	Matter–Mesnalty	March	1906
	Mesne–Misbirth	December	1906
	Misbode–Monopoly	June	1907
	Monopoly–Movement	March	1908
	Movement–Myz	September	1908
	N–Niche	September	1906
	Niche–Nywe	September	1907
Vol. VII.	O–Onomastic	July	1902
	Onomastical–Outing	March	1903
	Outjet–Ozyat	January	1904
	P–Pargeted	March	1904
	Pargeter–Pennached	December	1904
	Pennage–Pfennig	September	1905
	Ph–Piper	June	1906
	Piper–Polygenistic	March	1907
	Polygenous–Premious	December	1907

	Premisal–Prophesier	December	1908
	Prophesy–Pyxis	September	1909
Vol. VIII.	Q	October	1902
	R–Reactive	July	1903
	Reactively–Ree	July	1904
	Ree–Reign	March	1905
	Reign–Reserve	January	1906
	Reserve–Ribaldously	June	1908
	Ribaldric–Romanite	March	1909
	Romanity–Roundness	December	1909
	Round-nosed–Ryze	March	1910
	S–Sauce	June	1909
	Sauce-alone–Scouring	June	1910
	Scouring–Sedum	March	1911
	See–Senatory	December	1911
	Senatory–Several	September	1912
	Several–Shaster	June	1913
	Shastri–Shyster	March	1914
Vol. IX.	Si–Simple	December	1910
	Simple–Sleep	September	1911
	Sleep–Sniggle	June	1912
	Sniggle–Sorrow	March	1913
	Sorrow–Speech	December	1913
	Speech–Spring	September	1914
	Spring–Standard	March	1915
	Standard–Stead	September	1914
	Stead–Stillatim	June	1916
	Stillation–Stratum	December	1917
	Stratus–Styx	September	1919
	Su–Subterraneous	December	1914
	Subterraneously–Sullen	December	1915
	Sullen–Supple	January	1917
	Supple–Sweep	March	1918
	Sweep–Szmikite	September	1919
	T–Tealt	September	1910
	Team–Tezkere	June	1911
	Th–Thyzle	March	1912
Vol. X.	Ti–Tombac	December	1912

Tombal–Trahysh	June	1913
Traik–Trinity	June	1914
Trink–Turn-down	June	1915
Turndun–Tzirid	March	1916
U–Unforeseeable	October	1921
Unforeseeing–Unright	July	1924
Unright–Uzzle	July	1926
V–Verificative	October	1916
Verificatory–Visor	August	1917
Visor–Vywer	April	1920
W–Wash	October	1921
Wash–Wavy	May	1923
Wavy–Wezzon	August	1926
Wh–Whisking	May	1923
Whisking–Wilfulness	November	1924
Wilga–Wise	August	1926
Wise–Wyzen	April	1928
X Y Z	October	1921

APPENDIX B

The following list is made up of American works cited in the *Oxford English Dictionary*. The list includes, often in an abbreviated form, only such authors and titles as may not be readily recognized as American. The duplication occasionally found in the list will, it is believed, be helpful in the light of the form in which the citations actually occur in the Dictionary.

Abbott, C. C., Waste-land Wanderings.
Abbott, Jacob, Wallace: a Franconia Story.
Abbott, John S. C., Napoleon.
Adair, James, American Indians.
Adams, Andy, Log of a Cowboy.
Adams, Henry, John Randolph.
Alden, J., Intellectual Philosophy.
Aldrich, T. B., From Ponkapog to Pesth; Marjorie Daw; Prudence Palfrey; Story of a Bad Boy.
Alger, W. R., Solitudes of Nature and Man; Doctrine of a Future Life.

Alienist and Neurologist.
Allen, Joel A., American Bison.
Anthony's Photographic Bulletin.
Arena.
Argosy.
Army and Navy Journal.
Arr, E. H., New England Bygones.
Atwater, Lyman H., Elementary Logic.

Bailey, L. H., Lessons with Plants.
Baird, Spencer F., Birds of North America; Mammals of North America.
Baker, W. M., New Timothy.
Baldwin, John D., Prehistoric Nations.
Baldwin, Joseph G., Flush Times of Alabama and Miss.
Bancroft, George, Footprints of Time; History of the U.S.
Bancroft, Hubert H., History of Central America.
Banks, Eliz. L., Campaigns of Curiosity; Autobiography of a Newspaper Girl; Mystery of Frances Farrington.
Barlow, J., Columbiad; Conspiracy of Kings; Constitution of 1791; Oration 4th July 1787; Vision of Columbus.
Barry, Patrick, Fruit Garden.
Bartholow, Roberts, Treatise on Materia Medica.
Bartlett, John R., Mexican Boundary.
Bartlett, S. C., Egypt to Palestine.
Barton, W. P. C., Compendium floræ Philadelphicæ, Flora of North America; Vegetable Materia Medica of U.S.
Bartram, Wm., Travels through North and South Carolina.
Bates, Mrs. E. P., Old Salem.
Beard, G. M., Sea-sickness.
Beecher, H. W., Lectures on Preaching; Sermons.
Belknap, J., Tour to White Mountains; History of New Hampshire.
Belknap Papers.
Bell, Alexander G., Upon the Production of Sound.
Bellamy, Edward, Looking Backward.
Beverly, Robt., History of Virginia.
Bible Society Record.

'Billings, Josh', Josh Billings, his Sayings; His Book of Sayings.

Bishop, N. H., Voyage Paper Canoe; Four Months in a Sneak Box.

Bishop, W. H., House of a Merchant Prince.

Boardman, G. D., Creative Week.

Boker, Geo. H., Plays and Poems; Calaynos.

Bourke, J. G., Snake Dance of Moquis.

Bouvier, John, Law Dictionary.

Bowen, Francis, Treatise on Logic.

Brace, C. L., Gesta Christi; Home Life in Germany.

Brackenridge, H. H., Modern Chivalry.

Brackenridge, H. M., Journal of a Voyage; Views of Louisiana.

Bramwell, W. C., Wool-carder.

Bridge, Horatio, Personal Recollections.

Brigham, W. T., Guatemala.

Bristed, Chas. A., Five Years in an English University; Upper Ten Thousand.

Brooks, E., Philos. Arithmetic.

Brooks, Phillips, Candle of Lord.

Brooks, W. K., Oyster.

Brother Jonathan (see Neal, J.).

Brown, Chas. B., Volney's View of the Soil (trans.); Edgar Huntley.

Browne, Dan. J., American Poultry Yard.

Bumstead, Freeman J., Pathology.

Burnett, Mrs. F. H., Little Lord Fauntleroy.

Burr, Enoch F., Ad Fidem; Ecce Cœlum.

Burr, F., Vegetables of America.

Burritt, Elihu, Walk from London to Land's End.

Burroughs, John, Wake-Robin; Locusts and Wild-Honey; Winter Sunshine.

Burroughs, W. H., Treatise on Law of Taxation.

Bushnell, H., Work and Play; Sermons on Living Subjects; Forgiveness and Law; God in Christ; Moral Use of Dark Things; Sermons for the New Life; Vicarious Sacrifice; Women's Suffrage; Natural and Supernatural.

Butler, J. G., Bible-work.

Bynner, Edwin L., Agnes Surriage.
Byrne, Oliver, Handbook for the Artisan.

Calhoun, John C., Works.
Carlton, Robert, New Purchase.
Carrol, Charles, Journal.
Cartwright, P., Autobiography.
Carver, Jonathan, Travels; Treatise on Culture of Tobacco.
Cary, Alice, Ballads, Lyrics, and Hymns; Pictures of Country Life.
Chadwick, Henry, Base Ball Manual.
Channing, Edward, Town and County Government.
Chapman, A. W., Flora of Southern U.S.
Cheever, Geo. B., Wanderings of a Pilgrim.
Christian Union.
Chr. World.
Church, Benjamin, History King Philip's War.
Church, Wm. C., Life of John Ericsson.
Churchill, W., Crossing.
Clark, E. W., Life in Japan.
Clarke, E. H., Sex in Education.
Cohen, J. S., Diseases of the Throat.
Conway, M. D., Republican superst.; Demonology and Devil Lore; Earthward Pilgrimage.
Cook, Joseph, Boston Monday Lectures.
Cooke, J. P., New Chemistry.
Cooke, Rose T., Somebody's Neighbors.
Cosmopolitan.
Coues, Elliott, Birds of the North-West; Fur-bearing Animals; Key to North American Birds.
Coues and Allen, J. A., North American Rodentia.
Cozzens, Fred. S., Sparrowgrass Papers.
Crawford, F. M., Roman Singer; Doctor Claudius; Greifenstein; Mr. Isaacs; Saracinesca.
Critic, The.
Croker, Mrs. B. M., Mr. Jervis; Peggy of the Bartons; Proper Pride; Village Tales.
Croly, Mrs., Manual of Needlework.

Crosby, Howard, The Christian Preacher.
Cruse, C. F., Eusebius' Ecclesiastical History.
Cummins, Maria S., Lamplighter; El Fureidis; Haunted Hearts; Mabel Vaughan.
Curtis, Geo. T., Life of Buchanan.
Curtis, Geo. W., Lotos-eating; Nile Notes; Potiphar Papers.
Custer, Eliz. B., Tenting on Plains; 'Boots and Saddles'.
Cutler, Manasseh, Life Journal.

Dall, Wm. H., Later Prehistoric Man; Alaska and its Resources; Tribes of the Extreme North-West.
Dallas, Alex. J., Report of Cases.
Dana, James D., Crustacea; Corals and Coral Islands; Elements of Geology; Geology; Manual of Geology; Manual of Mineralogy; System of Mineralogy; Zoophytes.
Dana, Richard H., The Buccaneer.
Dana, Richard H., Jun., Seaman's Manual; Two Years before the Mast.
Darlington, Wm., Memorials of John Bartram; American Weeds.
Davies, Charles, Metric System.
Davies and Peck, W. G., Mathematical Dictionary.
Davis, Chas. A., Jack Downing.
Davis, Charles H., Narrative of the North Polar Expedition.
Davis, C. T., Manufacture of Leather; Manufacture of Bricks.
Davis, H., American Constitution.
Davis, R. H., Van Bibber; Our English Cousins.
De Kay, C., Vision of Nimrod.
De Kay, Jas. E., Zoology of New York.
Dialect Notes.
Dobbs, Arthur, Account of Countries.
Dodge, R. I., Hunting Grounds; Our Wild Indians.
Dolley, C. S., Technology of Bacteria.
Douglass, W., Summary.
'Dow, Jun.', Short Patent Sermons.
Draper, John W., History American Civil War; History Conflict between Religion and Science; History Intellectual Development; Human Physiology.

Duncan, Sara J., American Girl in London; A Social Departure.
Durivage, F. Alex., Stray Subjects.
Dwight, Timothy, Theology Explained; Travels in New England.

Eggleston, Edward, The Faith Doctor; The Graysons; Roxy; Transit of Civilization.
Ellicott, Andrew, Journal.
Elliott, H. W., Seal Islands of Alaska.
Ellis, John, The New Christianity.
Elton, Romeo, Life of Roger Williams.
Emerton, Jas. H., Common Spiders of U.S.
Erni, Henry, Mineralogy Simplified.
Evans, A. J., Through Bosnia.
Evans, Lewis, Geographical, Historical Essays.
Everett, Edward, Orations and Speeches.

Farragut, L., Life of D. G. Farragut.
Fawcett, E., Rutherford.
Felton, C. C., Ancient and Modern Greece; Familiar Letters.
Fessenden, Thom. G., Democracy Unveiled; Original Poems; Terrible Tractoration.
Fiske, John, Century of Science; Outlines of Cosmic Philosophy.
'Fleming, G.', Mirage.
Flint, Austin, Treatise on Principles and Practice of Medicine.
Flint, Jas., Letters from America.
Flint, Timothy, Condensed Geography and History; George Mason.
Forest and Stream.
Forney, M. N., Car-builder's Dictionary.

Galaxy Magazine.
Gass, Patrick, Journal.
Geikie, John C., English Reformation; George Stanley; Life and Works of Christ.
George, Henry, Progress and Poverty; Social Problems.
Georgia Scenes (see Longstreet, A. B.).
Gesner, Abraham, Treatise on Coal.
Gilder, Richard W., Poet and Master.

Gildersleeve, B. L., Essays and Studies.
Gilliam, A. M., Travels in Mexico.
Gilmore, John R. (see Kirke, E.)
Gist, C., Journals.
Gliddon, Geo. R., Ancient Egypt.
Goodale, Geo. L., Physiological Botany.
Goode, Geo. B., Menhaden; American Fishes; Fisheries; History of Fisheries; Review of Fishing; Fishes of Bermudas.
Goodrich, Sam. G., Recollections of Lifetime.
Gould, Geo. M., New Medical Dictionary.
Goulding, Francis R., Young Marooners.
Gray, Asa, Manual of Botany; First Lessons in Botany; Botanical text-book.
Green, Anna K., Behind Closed Doors; Hand and Ring.
Greenleaf, A. B., Ten Years in Texas.
Gunter, A. C., Miss Dividends; That Frenchman.

Habberton, J., My Friend Moses; Helen's Babies.
Hadley, J., Essays; Greek Grammar.
Hale, Edward E., Christmas in Palace; Christmas in Narragansett; His Level Best; How to do it; In His Name; Ups and Downs; Ten Times One.
Hale, Edward E. (the younger), James Russell Lowell.
Haliburton, Thomas C., Clockmaker; Nature and Human Nature.
Hall, B. H., College Words.
Hall, F., Modern English; English Adjectives; Rational Refutation Hindu Philosophy; Exemplifications of False Philology.
Hall, Jas., Legends of the West; Notes on Western States.
Hall, John, A Christian Home.
Hamilton, Allan McL., Nervous Diseases.
Hammond, Sam. H., Hunting Adventures.
Hammond, Wm. A., Diseases of Nervous System.
Harlan, Geo. C., Eyesight.
'Harland, Marion', Alone; Common Sense; Hidden Path.
Harris, Thaddeus W., Insects Injurious to Vegetation.

Hart, A. B., Formation of the Union.

Hawthorne, Julian, Dust; Fortune's Fool; Garth; The Laughing Mill; Nathaniel Hawthorne.

Hay, John, Pike County Ballads; Bread-winners.

Henry, A., Travels.

Henry, J. J., Campaign against Quebec.

Henshall, Jas. A., Camping and Cruising in Florida.

Herman, H., His Angel.

Hickok, Laurens P., Mental Science.

Higginson, Thos. W., Oldport Days; Malbone; Young Folks' History.

Hill, D. J., Bryant.

Hill, T., True Order Studies.

Hinsdale, Burke A., Garfield and Education.

Hitchcock, Edward, Ichnology of New England.

Hodgson, Fred T., Stair-building made Easy.

Hoffman, C. F., Greyslaer.

Holbrook, M. L., Hygiene of the Brain.

Holder, C. F., Marvels of Animal Life.

Holland, Josiah G., Marble Prophecy; Arthur Bonnicastle; Bay-path; Gold-foil; History Western Massachusetts; Kathrina; Lessons in Life; Letters; Life of Lincoln; Mistress of the Manse; Plain Talk; Sevenoaks; Timothy Titcomb's Letters; Miss Gilbert's Career.

Homans, Isaac S., Cyclopedia of Commerce.

Homiletic Monthly.

Hooper, Night at Ugly Man's.

Horton, S. Dana, Silver and Gold.

Hosmer, Jas. K., Short History of Anglo-Saxon Freedom.

Hubbard, Wm., Narrative; Happiness of a People; Present State of New England; History of Indian Wars.

Hughes, G., Natural History of Barbados.

Humphreys, David, Miscellaneous Works; Poems; Yankey in England.

Hunter, J. D., Memoirs of a Captivity.

Hutchinson, Thomas, Diary; History of Massachusetts.

Ingraham, Jos. H., Pillar of Fire.

Jackson, Helen Hunt, Sonnets and Lyrics; Verses.

James, Henry, Daisy Miller; Bostonians; Europeans; A Little Tour in France; Madonna of the Future; Passionate Pilgrim; Portrait of a Lady; Roderick Hudson; Tales of Three Cities; Tragic Muse; Transatlantic Sketches; London Life; Diary of a Man of Fifty.

James, Wm., Pragmatism; Principles of Psychology; Varieties of Religious Experience.

Jewett, Sarah O., Deephaven; A Country Doctor; Tales of New England.

Johnson, Edward, History of New England, or Wonder-Working Providence.

Johnson, Oliver, W. Lloyd Garrison.

Johnson, W., Reports.

Jordan and Gilbert, Synopsis Fishes of North America.

Judd, S., Margaret.

Kane, Elisha K., Arctic Explorations; U. S. Grinnell Expedition.

Kendall, G. W., Texan Santa Fé Expedition.

Kennedy, J. P., Horse-Shoe Robinson; Memoirs of Life of Wm. Wirt; Swallow-Barn; Annals of Quodlibet; Rob of the Bowl.

Kent, Jas., Commentaries on American Law.

Kimball, R. B., Was he Successful? Undercurrents of Wall-street.

King, Chas., Mountaineering.

Kingsley, John S. (ed.), Standard Natural History (reissued as Riverside Natural History).

Kirk, John F., History of Chas. the Bold.

'Kirke, E.', Garfield.

Kirkland, Mrs., Forest Life.

Knapp, M. L., Astronomical Etiology.

Knapp, Wm. I., Life of George Barrow.

Knight, Edward H., Dictionary of Mechanics.

Knight, Henry C., Letters from South and West.

Ladd, Geo. T., Elements of Physiological Psychology; Introduction to Philosophy; Outlines Physiological Psychology; Philosophy of Knowledge; Theory of Reality.

Langille, J. H., Our Birds in their Haunts.
Lea, M. Carey, Photography.
Le Conte, Jos., Classif. Lepidoptera North America; Elements of Geology; Religion and Science; Sight.
Lee, A. E., History of City of Columbus.
Leland, Chas. G., Abraham Lincoln; Egyptian Sketch-Book; Memoirs; Pidgin-English Sing-Song.
Library Magazine.
Lippincott's Magazine.
Literary World.
Littell's Living Age.
Lockwood, Thom. D., Electricity, Magnetism, and Electric Telegraph.
Longstreet, A. B., Georgia Scenes.
Loomis, E., Treatise on Astronomy.
Lossing, B. J., The Hudson.
Lounsbury, Thom. R., Studies in Chaucer.
Ludlow, Fitz H., Little Brother.
Lumberman's Gazette.

MacCook, Henry C., American Spiders.
Macsparran, J., America Dissected; Letter Book and Abstract.
McClure, A. K., Rocky Mountains.
Mahan, Alfred T., Influence of Sea Power; Lessons of War with Spain.
Major Jack Downing.
Major Jones Courtship.
Mann, Edward C., Psychological Medicine.
March, Francis A., Anglo-Saxon Grammar.
Marcy, R. B., Prairie Traveller; Border Reminiscences.
Marsh, G. P., Man and Nature; Lectures on Language.
Masque of Poets.
Mathews, Geo. D., Coinage.
Mathews, W., Words; Getting on in the World.
Matthews, W., Ethnography: Hidatsa Indians.
Maury, M. F., Phys. Geography of Sea.
Maynard, C. J., Birds of Florida.
Mayo, Wm. S., Kaloolah; Never Again.

Medical News.
Meigs, J. A., Observations on Cranial Forms.
Melville, Herman, Moby Dick; Omoo; White Jacket.
Menken, Adah I, Infelicia.
Merriam, Geo. S., Life of S. Bowles.
Miller, 'Joaquin', Songs of Italy; Songs of the Sierras; Memorie and Rime.
Millspaugh, Chas. F., American Medical Plants.
Mitchell, Donald G., Seven Stories; Battle Summer; Bound Together; Dream Life; The Lorgnette; Reveries of a Bachelor; Wet Days at Edgewood.
Morgan, Lewis H., Ancient Society.
Morris, Geo. P., Poems.
Morris, Gouv., Spark's Life.
Morse, E. S., Japanese Homes.
Morse, J. F., Jun., John Q. Adams.
Murphy, J. G., Commentary on Genesis; Commentary on Exodus; Commentary on Leviticus.

Napheys, Geo. H., Prevention and Cure of Disease.
Nation, The.
Neal, J., Brother Jonathan.
Neal, Joseph C., Charcoal Sketches.
Neidé, C. A., Canoe Aurora.
Newcomb, Simon, Popular Astronomy.
Newcomb and Holder, Astronomy.
New Virginians.
Nichols, Jas. R., Fireside Science.
Niles Register.
Noble, Louis L., Icebergs.
Noel, Edward H., Richter's Flower, Fruit, and Thorn Pieces (trans.).
Nordhoff, Chas., Communistic Societies of the U.S.
Norton, C. E., Letters; Divine Comedy (trans.); Historical Studies of Church Building.

Olcott, Henry S., Posthumous Humanity (trans.); Theosophy.
Olmsted, Fred L., Journey through Texas; Cotton Kingdom;

Englishman in Kansas; Journey in Back Country; Journey in Slave States.
O'Reilly, H., Fifty Years on the Trail.
Orton, Jas., Andes and the Amazon.
Outing.

Palmer, Joel, Journal of Travels.
Parker, T., Works; Experience as a Minister; Historic Americans; Sermons.
Paulding, Jas. K., Letters from South.
Peaslee, Edmund R., Ovarian Tumors.
Penhallow, Sam., Indian Wars; Penitential Confession.
Perkins, Chas. C., Handbook Italian Sculpture; Italian Sculptors.
Perkins, J., Eight Years' Residence in Persia.
Perry, Arthur L., Elements of Political Economy.
Peter Parley's Annual.
Peterson's Magazine.
Phelps, Austin, The Still Hour.
Phelps, Eliz. S., Hedged in; Sealed Orders; Silent Partner.
Phillips, H., American Paper Currency; Chamisso's Faust (trans.); Notes upon Collection of Coins.
Phillips, W., Speeches.
Pickering, Chas., Chronological History of Plants.
Pope, Frank L., Modern Practice Electric Telegraph.
Popular Science Monthly.
Porter, N., Human Intellect; American Colleges.
Porter, Wm. T., Quarter Race in Kentucky; (ed.) Big Bear of Arkansas, &c.
Preble, George H., Our Flag.
Prentiss, Mrs. E. B., Life and Letters.
Prescott, Geo. B., Speaking Telephone; History Electric Telegraph.
Pumpelly, Raphael, Across America and Asia.
Putnam, A. A., Ten Years Police Judge.

Quincy, Josiah P., Figures of the Past.

Raymond, Rossiter W., Glossary of Mining; Statistics of Mines.
Redfield, J. F., Law Railway.

Reed, H., Lectures.
Remsen, Ira, Introduction to Organic Chemistry.
Riverside Natural History.
Robb, John S., Streaks of Squatter Life.
Roe, Edward P., Nature's Serial Story.
Rogers, H. D., Geology.
Rollins, Mrs. E. C., New England Bygones.
Roosa, Daniel B., Diseases of the Ear.
Roosevelt, B., Copper Queen.
Root, Jesse, Report of Cases.
Russell, Wm. C., Curatica; Death Ship; Good Ship 'Mohock'; Jack's Courtship; John Holdsworth; Marooned; A Marriage at Sea; Ocean free-lance; Ocean Tragedy; Sailors' Language; Sailor's Sweetheart; Sea Queen; What Cheer; Wreck of the 'Grosvenor'.
Ruxton, Geo. F., Adventures in Mexico; Life in Far West.

Saltus, Edgar E., Madame Sapphira.
Sanborn, Kate, A Truthful Woman.
Sargent, W., Braddock's Expedition.
Say, Thomas, American Entomology.
Scammon, Chas. M., Marine Mammals.
Schaff, Philip, Encyclopedia Religious Knowledge; Christ and Christianity; History Christian Church.
Schley, Winfield S., Rescue of Greely.
Schoolcraft, Henry R., Narrative of an Expedition; Historical and Statistical Information.
Scidmore, Eliz. R., Alaska.
Sears, Edmund H., Athanasia; The Fourth Gospel; Regeneration; Sermons and Songs.
Sears, G. W., Woodcraft; Forest Runes.
Sedgwick, C. M., Live and Let Live; The Linwoods; Letters from Abroad; Hope Leslie.
Sewall, Sam., Diary; Letter Book.
Shedd, Wm. G. T., Dogmatic Theology; History of Christian Doctrine.
Shepard, Chas. U., Treatise on Mineralogy.
Sheridan, Philip H., Personal Memoirs.

Shields, Chas. W., Final Philosophy.
Sill, E. R., Hermitage and Other Poems.
Silliman, Benj., Remarks on a Tour.
Silliman, Benj., Jun., Principles of Physics.
'Slick, Jonathan', High Life in New York.
Smith, Chas. F., On Southernisms.
Smith, Seba, Life of Jack Downing.
Sparrow, Wm., Select Discourses.
Spofford, Harriet, Pilot's Wife; Amber Gods; Sir Rohan's Ghost.
Squier, Ephraim G., Notes on Central America; Peru, Incidents of Travel.
Stanley, H. M., Through the Dark Continent; The Congo; In Darkest Africa.
Stephens, J. L., Incidents of Travel.
Stockton, Frank R., Dusantes; Lady or Tiger? Rudder Grange.
Stoddard, R. H., Poems.
Story, W. W., Roba di Roma.
Stuart, Ruth M., In Simpkinsville.
Sullivan, Jas., History of Maine.
Sumner, C., Memoirs and Letters; Orations and Speeches.

Talmage, T. De Witt, Crumbs Swept Up; Jewels of the Soul; Sermons.
Taylor, B., Northern Travel; Critical Essays; Eldorado, Goethe's Faust (trans.); Hannah Thurston; Pictures of Palestine; Poems; Prince Deukalion; Studies in German Literature.
Taylor, G. H., Pelvic and Hernial Therapeutics.
Thayer, W. M., Log Cabin to White House.
Thomas, Theodore G., Diseases of Women.
Thompson, Wm. T., Major Jones's Courtship.
Thorpe, T. B., Mysteries of Backwoods.
Thurston, R. H., Steam Engine.
Ticknor, Geo., History Spanish Literature; Life W. H. Prescott; Life, Letters, and Journals.
Tidball, John C., Manual of Heavy Artillery Service.

Tomes, Robert, Americans in Japan.
Tourgee, Albion W., Fool's Errand.
Townsend, M., United States.
Trumbull, J., McFingal; Poetical Works.
Tuckerman, Henry T., The Collector.
Tuttle, Edmund B., Border Tales.
Tyler, Moses C., Glimpses of England; History of American Literature.

Uncle Philip's Conversations.

Van Buren, W. H., Diseases.
Voice, The.

Walker, Francis A., Text-book Political Economy; Land and its Rent; Money; Political Economy.
Wallack, L., Memoirs.
Warner, C. D., Backlog Studies; Their Pilgrimage; Saunterings; Roundabout Journey; In the Levant; Mummies and Moslems; My Winter on the Nile; Washington Irving.
Washburn, Emory, Treatise on American Law.
Wayland, Francis, Life of Adoniram Judson.
Weeden, W. B., Social Law of Labor.
Weems, Mason L., Life of Washington.
Weiss, J., Wit, Humor, and Shakespeare.
Welby, A., Poems.
Welcker, Adair, Tales of 'Wild and Woolly West'.
Westcott, Edward N., David Harum.
Wheaton, Nathaniel S., Journal of a Residence.
Wheeler, D. H., By-ways of Literature.
Whipple, E. P., Essays and Reviews; Character and Characteristic men; Success and its Conditions.
Whitcher, Frances M., Widow Bedott Papers.
White, Richard C., England Without and Within; Every-day English; Studies in Shakespeare; Words and their Uses; Fate of Mansfield Humphries.
White, S. E., Riverman; Blazed Trail.
Whitney, Mrs. A. D., A Summer in L. Goldthwaite's Life;

Other Girls; Sights and Insights; Gayworthys; Odd or Even? F. Gartney's Girlhood; We Girls; Patience Strong's Outings.

Whitney, J. D., Names and Places; Metalic Wealth of the U.S.

Whitney, W. D., English Grammar; Language and the Study of Language; Life and Growth of Language; Oriental and Linguistic Studies.

Wilkins, Mary, Humble Romance; The Love of Parson Lord.

Willis, N. P., Lady Jane; Melanie, and other Poems; Pencillings by the Way; Poems; Poems of Early and After Years; Sketches; Summer Cruise.

Winchell, A., World-life; Walks and Talks; Reconciliation of Science and Religion.

Winsor, J., Cartier to Frontenac; Christopher Columbus; Mississippi Basin.

Winthrop, T., Cecil Dreeme; E. Brotherloft; Canoe and Saddle.

Wirt, Wm., Sketches of Life of Patrick Henry.

Wood, Alphonso, American Botanist; Class-book of Botany.

Wood, H. C., Freshwater Algæ; Treatise on Therapeutics.

Woolman, John, Journal.

Woolson, C. F., For the Major; Anne; Jupiter Lights.

Young, C. A., Uranography; The Sun.

Young, J. J., Ceramic Art.

INDEX

INDEX